CW00670194

EVERYTHING IS
MNÁSOME

First published in 2024 by The O'Brien Press Ltd,
12 Terenure Road East, Rathgar, Dublin 6, D06 HD27 Ireland.
Tel: +353 1 4923333; Fax: +353 1 4922777
E-mail: books@obrien.ie; Website: obrien.ie
The O'Brien Press is a member of Publishing Ireland.

ISBN: 978-1-78849-533-2

Text © copyright Kunak McGann, 2024
The moral rights of the author have been asserted.
Copyright for typesetting, layout, editing, design © The O'Brien Press Ltd
Cover design and internal design by Emma Byrne

All rights reserved. No part of this publication may be reproduced or utilised in any
form or by any means, electronic or mechanical, including for text and data mining,
training artificial intelligence systems, photocopying, recording or in any information
storage and retrieval system, without permission in writing from the publisher.

8 7 6 5 4 3 2 1
28 27 26 25 24

Printed and bound by and bound by Hussar Books.
The paper in this book is produced using pulp from managed forests.

Author's note:
*I have been as accurate as possible in assigning dates, though a small number of events could
only be narrowed down to within a few days or, in some cases, to specific months. I hope
that readers will forgive this poetic licence.*

Published in

EVERYTHING IS
MNÁSOME

365 Days of Celebrating Irish Women

Kunak McGann

THE O'BRIEN PRESS
DUBLIN

Acknowledgements

As I grow older, I realise how lucky I am to have a life filled with the most interesting, inspirational, fierce and funny women. My heartfelt thanks to my mum and sister, mother-in-law, sisters-in-law, cousins, aunts and nieces, and good friends, especially my weekenders and book clubbers who make me laugh so much.

And to the amazing women I've worked with in publishing, from the femtastic OBP crew – past and present – to the army of writers and illustrators who fearlessly put themselves out there. Special thanks to my editor, Nicola Reddy, who is brilliant of course, but always just 'gets' me, and Emma Byrne, for really smashing it with this cover.

For Mum and for my sister, Erika,
the most mnásome women
I know.

Introduction

When I first suggested this idea for a book – a celebration of Irish women for every date in the year – I was very pleased with myself. That feeling lasted only as long as it took me to get stuck into allocating dates. What I had created for myself was a jigsaw puzzle for which there might not be connecting pieces. But the more I went down the rabbit hole of internet research, the more obsessed I became with learning about these women. For every icon I had a date for – Constance Markievicz, Mary Robinson and Sinéad O'Connor – there were other, less well-known women like Nancy Corrigan, Dorothy Stopford Price or Kate Kennedy blazing a trail in their own ways. And of course, there were far more extraordinary women than there were dates in the year.

When Elizabeth Blackburne put together the first anthology of biographies of Irish women in the 1870s, she called it 'the silent patriotism of my life'. While this little book is not nearly on that scale, by the time I had finished it, I was a prouder Irish person and a prouder feminist. My hope is that these little tasters will serve as inspiration to find out more about the many, many Irish women who have made this world a better place.

JANUARY

1ˢᵗ **January** 2012

Dr Rhona Mahony became master of the National Maternity Hospital in Holles Street. She was the first woman to head up an Irish maternity hospital. During her term, she oversaw the care of ten thousand pregnant women – and their little bundles of joy – every year.

2ⁿᵈ **January** 1945

An extract from Mary Lavin's debut novel, *The House in Clewe Street*, appeared in *The Atlantic* magazine in the US. Born in Massachusetts, Mary moved back to Ireland at the age of nine. Her many novels and short stories centred on women's lives – her stories on widowhood are thought to be some of her best. In 2021, she was the first Irish female writer to have a public space named after her. You can now take a stroll down to Mary Lavin Place near Dublin's Grand Canal.

3rd January 2001

Dublin journalist Orla Guerin was appointed the BBC's Middle East correspondent, based in Jerusalem. Her award-winning career began in Ireland when she joined RTÉ as their youngest ever foreign correspondent – she was posted to Eastern Europe at just twenty-three years old. Cool under fire (literally), she has reported from the likes of Kosovo, Johannesburg and Haiti.

4th January 2018

The first episode of sitcom *Derry Girls* was broadcast on Channel 4, and it was love at first 'Catch yourself on!' With razor-sharp writing by Lisa McGee and a truckload of 90s nostalgia, we all adored the gang of teen misfits. The show ran for three seasons, catapulting the actors to full-blown stardom. It won an Emmy, and BAFTAs for Lisa's writing and Siobhán McSweeney's brilliantly sardonic portrayal of Sr Michael. *giant eyeroll*

5th January 1927

Roscommon teacher Margaret 'Gretta' Cousins founded the All India Women's Conference to empower and educate women. At home, Gretta was a fierce campaigner for Ireland's independence and women's rights, and she continued her mission after moving to India in 1915. She was imprisoned in three different countries for political protest: in Ireland and Britain for suffrage activities, and in India in support of Gandhi.

6th January

Nollaig na mBan or Women's Christmas is an Irish celebration getting a welcome new lease of life. It was traditionally a day for women to put their feet up after the work of the festive season. They would meet in each other's houses for a cup of tea and a bite of Christmas cake. With household duties more evenly spread these days (you'd hope), it's a chance to celebrate the amazing women in our lives. Did somebody say 'girls night out'?

7th January 1966

Mary Finn from Sligo was the first female winner of the Young Scientist exhibition. Bucking the stereotype, she used complex maths to tackle the 'Four Colour Problem' (that it only takes four colours on a map to avoid having two neighbouring countries of the same colour). She later put her smarts to good use by becoming a science teacher.

8th January 2008

Cork native Dr Clare O'Leary became the first Irish woman to ski to the South Pole. She was also the first Irish woman to reach the top of Mount Everest and to climb the Seven Summits, the highest mountains on each continent. Those of us with tamer aspirations – and frankly, less energy – can honour her by trying the popular Clare O'Leary Walk between Bandon and Innishannon.

9th January 2003

The news was out: twenty-one-year-old Cecelia Ahern had secured herself a 'million-dollar book deal'. Her debut novel, *PS I Love You*, was a huge international hit the following year. The Dubliner has been a regular on the bestseller lists ever since, with a new offering almost every year. She has sold a stonking twenty-five million copies in thirty languages worldwide.

10th January 1877

Eliza Walker Dunbar was the first woman in Ireland or Britain to obtain a medical licence. Travelling over from Scotland, Dunbar took her exams at the only university that would let her: King and Queen's (now the Royal) College of Physicians in Ireland. The year before, new equality legislation was passed in Westminster, and this Dublin college was the first in the United Kingdom to step up. It was a breakthrough in the fight for women doctors.

11th January 2024

Blinne Ní Ghrálaigh gave a blistering closing statement in the International Court of Justice as she and her team made the case against Israel for Palestinian genocide. The Mayo-born lawyer specialises in international law and human rights, and she previously worked on the Bloody Sunday Inquiry and the Croatia-Serbia genocide case. She saw firsthand the conditions in Gaza on a fact-finding trip.

12th January 2018

Deborah Somorin appeared on RTÉ's *The Late Late Show* to share her experience of homelessness. Living in a hostel at thirteen and pregnant at fourteen, Deborah tragically lost her mother, who took her own life. Now a successful management consultant, she founded Empower the Family to help disadvantaged students. Her vision earned her a place on the *Forbes* '30 Under 30' list.

13th January 1964

After twenty-four years of men only, Jane 'Jennie' Dowdall was the first woman appointed to the Irish Council of State, where she remained the only woman for over a decade. A trained nurse, she was Cork's first woman mayor. She was a great patron of the arts and used her influence to secure funding for the Cork Opera House.

14th January 2019

Sindy Joyce donned her cap and gown to receive her PhD from the University of Limerick. She was the first Traveller – or Mincéir in her own language, Cant – to earn a doctorate. From Newcastle West, Sindy had carried out her sociological research on young Travellers' experiences of racism in urban spaces. Dr Joyce was appointed to the Council of State later that year.

15th January 1912

Sarah Cecilia Harrison topped the poll to become the first woman elected to Dublin City Council. A leading portrait artist, the County Down woman helped establish the Hugh Lane Gallery. As a councillor, she fought for equal pay for women and relief work for the unemployed. The Dublin trades council called her 'the noblest, bravest and most accomplished woman in Ireland'.

16th January 1891

One of the first women in Ireland to qualify as a doctor, Mary Hannan was recruited to run the Dufferin women's hospital in Agra, India. A real progressive, the Dubliner was a strong proponent of sex education. In later life, she lived in South Africa and point-blank refused to pay its 'super-bachelor tax' on single women (but not men). She was described as a 'champion of the unmarried ladies'. Too right.

17th January 1886

Cousins Edith Somerville and Violet Martin met for the first time on this day and soon began writing together as 'Somerville and Ross'. They published more than a dozen social satire novels – their most popular was later adapted for TV as *The Irish R.M.* Violet died more than thirty years before her cousin, but Edith would continue to write under their joint pen name. The pair are buried side by side.

18th January 2002

The acclaimed biopic of the Dublin-born writer Iris Murdoch, *Iris*, opened in cinemas. Iris published twenty-six novels on morality, sexual relationships and life versus art. Nominated for the Booker Prize an impressive seven times, she won in 1978 for *The Sea, The Sea*. She once said, 'I think being a woman is like being Irish … Everyone says you're important and nice, but you take second place all the same.'

19th January 1865

Upon the death of her husband, Ellen Jane Corrigan became CEO of the Bushmills whiskey distillery in all but name. A shrewd businesswoman, she modernised the County Antrim company for a world market. She introduced electricity, massively bumped up production, and set up a limited company. When she sold it fifteen years later, she retained a seat on the company board – unheard of for a woman at the time.

20th January 1848

The good ship *Garrick* docked in New York after a forty-day voyage from Liverpool. Thirty-three babies were born during the journey, including a little girl called Bridget, born to mother Anne Kerny. During the Famine years, eight thousand babies were born on the coffin ships to New York. Women fled Ireland to give birth in the dark, airless and fetid conditions of steerage passengers. Incredible courage and endurance.

21st January 1974

French footie club Stade de Reims signed seventeen-year-old Dubliner Anne O'Brien. Technically, France didn't allow professional women footballers, so Anne was contracted as a part-time factory worker. She went on to play in the Italian league, winning six titles and playing to fifty-thousand–strong crowds. When her son was born, she returned to play after just four weeks, breastfeeding him in the dressing room at half-time.

22nd January 1904

Isabel Marion Weir Johnston arrived in Dublin, the first woman to be admitted to Trinity College as a student. She and forty other women on campus were not allowed attend lectures, use the canteen or be present on the grounds after 6pm. Marion organised dances and tennis tournaments and founded the Elizabethan Society (the Eliz) for debating. (The university's other debating societies wouldn't admit women until the 1960s – for shame!). Trinity's former provost George Salmon said that 'over my dead body will women enter the college'. Ironically, he died the day Marion arrived in Dublin. Her examination had to be delayed til after his funeral.

23rd January 1834

Mother Mary Aikenhead founded St. Vincent's Hospital at St. Stephen's Green, the first hospital in Ireland or Britain to be managed and staffed entirely by women. Mary was known for her immense energy and passion. When confined to bed with spinal problems, she wrote more than four thousand letters asking for hospital donations. What someone like her could have done with the power of email and social media …

24th January 2017

Ruth Negga landed her first Oscar nomination for her portrayal of the real-life Mildred Loving. Ruth was born in Addis Ababa and grew up in Limerick. After a number of roles in homegrown productions including *Love/Hate*, Hollywood came a-calling. Talking about on-screen characters, Ruth once said, 'I don't know why women aren't allowed to have the same sort of breadth and scope and flaws of men. It kinda nags at me, you know?' We know exactly.

25th January 1990

Sinéad O'Connor's heartrending version of 'Nothing Compares 2 U' topped the Irish charts. One of the country's most talented singer-songwriters, her acclaimed album *I Do Not Want What I Haven't Got* sold over seven million copies. A defiant human rights activist, she sparked outrage in 1992 when protesting clerical sex abuse by ripping up a photo of the Pope on *Saturday Night Live*. Sinéad's death in 2023 was met with a national and international outpouring of grief.

26th January 1907

Riots broke out at the opening night of J. M. Synge's *The Playboy of the Western World* at the Abbey Theatre in Dublin. The crowd was appalled by the word 'shift', meaning a modest piece of women's underwear. The rioters were applauded by the *Irish Independent* for their good taste and common sense. One can only imagine what they would have made of *The Vagina Monologues*.

27th January 1942

Sheila Tinney had her first scientific paper published, based on her PhD research on crystal lattices. She was a gifted physicist and the first Irish woman to earn a doctorate in mathematical science. Born and raised in Galway, Sheila was one of only eight girls to tackle Honours Maths the year she sat her Leaving Cert. She went on to lecture in UCD, developing their first course on quantum mechanics and inspiring generations of students.

28th January 2024

The final episode of *Second Chances*, hosted by Ireland's first trans TV presenter, was broadcast. Rebecca Tallon De Havilland was shockingly outed as a trans woman on the front page of an Irish newspaper thirty years ago. Following her diagnosis with HIV and a hard-fought battle with addiction, she published her landmark memoir in 2010. She is a trailblazing activist on trans rights and HIV awareness.

29th January 2015

Anne Enright was named Ireland's inaugural Laureate for Irish Fiction. The Dubliner's talent had been recognised right from her first book, *The Portable Virgin*, which scooped the Rooney Prize. Her fourth novel, *The Gathering*, was awarded the Booker. She once mused that 'If you grow up in Ireland and read books then you really are obliged to attempt your own some time.'

30th January 1995

On this day, the government increased maternity leave to eighteen weeks. It would be increased again a decade later to the current twenty-six weeks. Ireland introduced maternity leave back in 1981, but we still lag behind many of our European sisters on maternity pay. If you live in Bulgaria, you can expect to be paid 90% of your full salary.

31st January 1881

Wicklow sisters Anna and Fanny Parnell set up the Ladies' Land League in Dublin. When the male leaders of the Land League were imprisoned, the women's league took over – and to much better effect. They opened five hundred branches countrywide and distributed £60,000 in relief funds (equivalent to millions today). The Archbishop of Dublin accused them of forgetting 'the modesty of their sex and the high dignity of their womanhood' – which only spurred them on. Of the two sisters, Anna was much more radical and militant. She would inspire the next generation of women activists.

FEBRUARY

1st February

The celebration day for Ireland's female patron saint. For many of us, St. Brigid is symbolised by the handmade reed crosses we hacked together in art class. But she was a 5th century feminist, a formidable abbess who didn't shrink from dealing with men in power. She brokered peace, freed trafficked women and negotiated property rights. She is the patron saint of cattle, dairymaids, blacksmiths, midwives and newborns, nuns, and brewing. Not necessarily in that order.

2nd February 2024

Figures showed that Ireland's gender pay gap had shrunk to about 8% for larger employers, the lowest ever. This fits with the clear trend in the overall workforce over the last fifteen years. Onwards and downwards!

3rd **February** 2014

Two days after Panti Bliss's Noble Call, an amazing
200,000 people had watched it online. The stirring
speech by Ireland's best-known drag queen was
a response to 'Pantigate', in which her alter-ego,
Rory O'Neill, had accused a number of people of
homophobia during an appearance on RTÉ. The
national broadcaster subsequently made a payout of
€85,000 to those named. In response to the ensuing
uproar, Panti's Noble Call went viral. It gave her
huge influence in the run-up to the 2015 marriage
referendum. Long live the Queen.

4th **February** 1914

The acclaimed portraitist Sarah Purser joined the board
of the National Gallery. Her portraits included many
of the most interesting personalities of the day. She had
no problem winning prestigious commissions: 'I went
through the British aristocracy like the measles.' Sarah

was seventy-five years old before the Royal Hibernian Academy would allow her as their first woman member. That same year, 1923, she had her first solo exhibition.

5th February 1976

The new Juries Act was passed in the Seanad. It would make women as eligible as men for jury duty for the first time since 1927. Many men (including those in power) felt that women shouldn't be subjected to the horrors of the criminal courts. Women's rights activists pointed out that they were already being exposed as lawyers, witnesses and defendants. And also, we could take it. It took half a century, but the Supreme Court finally agreed.

6th February 1918

The Representation of the People Act gave the vote to women in Ireland and Britain. Women who were over the age of thirty, that is. And university graduates.

Or landowners. Or wives of landowners. It was a huge victory for the suffrage movement, but many of the women campaigners were left without the vote. There was still some way to go.

7th February 1960

The Irish League of Credit Unions was founded by Nora Herlihy. The Cork woman had always had a passion for helping those with less. She set up Ireland's first credit union in Dublin's Donore Avenue, and later the national body – all while working full-time as a teacher. And it turned out, the Irish were mad for the credit unions. A whopping three quarters of us have accounts in our local branch.

8th February 2024

Aeronautical engineer Dr Norah Patten addressed thousands of teenagers at the I WISH conference in Dublin. I WISH was created to encourage girls' interest in science, technology, engineering and maths (STEM). When Norah was just eleven years old, a visit to a NASA research centre ignited a lifelong interest in space. Since then, the Mayo native has undergone astronaut training, spacesuit testing, high-g and microgravity flight. In 2024, it was officially announced that she would be our first ever astronaut – boldly going where no-one (Irish) has gone before.

9th February 2020

Eimear Noone was the first woman to conduct the orchestra at the Oscars ceremony. The Galwegian has won awards for conducting and composing musical scores for video games like *The Legend of Zelda* and *World of Warcraft*. She was the first woman conductor at Dublin's National Concert Hall. Making music and breaking records.

10th February 2004

NUI announced Alice Leahy as the recipient of an honorary doctorate. A former nurse and midwife, Alice helped set up the first Intensive Care Unit in Baggot Street Hospital. She co-founded the Alice Leahy Trust in 1975 and oversaw its running for forty years. It offers homeless people shelter, fresh clothes, warm showers – and no judgement.

11th February 2024

Athlete Rhasidat Adeleke broke her own indoor record for the 300m. She then held no less than six national records, including the first woman to break 50 seconds in the 400m. Born in Dublin to Nigerian parents, Rhasidat trained with Tallaght Athletic Club from the age of twelve. She had a meteoric rise up the rankings and, at just twenty-one, was the first Irish woman to reach an Olympic sprint final. Watch this space.

12th February 2015

Lynn Ruane began her political career at the age of thirty as president of Trinity Students' Union. Growing up in Tallaght, Lynn left school when she became a single mother at fifteen. She later returned to education, first studying addiction, then politics and philosophy at Trinity. She was elected a senator in 2016. She insists that 'feminism is leaving large groups of women behind … There is no progression without equity.'

13th February 2014

The *Connacht Tribune* published an historic interview with Tuam native Catherine Corless. Catherine's painstaking research revealed missing burial records for large numbers of children in the Bon Secours Mother and Baby Home. On foot of her work, the remains of hundreds of babies were discovered inside a disused waste tank on the Tuam premises. The publication of her research was a watershed moment for Irish society.

14th February 1910

The Royal Irish Academy discussed its first application for full membership from a woman, 'a widow lady'. It was rejected on legal advice – the society's charter ruled out married women members, and likely single ones too. It would be nearly forty years before women were admitted to the RIA. Four women became members in 1949, including scientists Sheila Tinney and Phyllis Clinch.

15th February 1946

One of the world's first digital computers, ENIAC, was unveiled. It had been programmed by half a dozen women – known as 'human computers' – including Donegal-born Kay McNulty. Kay was a maths genius who had been recruited by the US Army to calculate ballistics trajectories. When she married a widower with two children, he gifted her a cookbook with the words, 'You are our new cook'. Kay cooked, raised seven children, and still found time to programme (uncredited) the computers her husband developed.

16th February 1896

Rosa Barrett's expert opinion on child welfare was sought for a study on Irish society. Rosa had moved to Dublin from England as a child. In a sign of things to come, she used her pocket money to pay a nurse to mind the families of local charwomen. She went on to found Dublin's first crèche, for mothers on low incomes. She also set up the Irish section of the National Society for the Prevention of Cruelty to Children (NSPCC).

17th February 2011

Teenager Joanne O'Riordan challenged Taoiseach Enda Kenny on the campaign trail. She objected to the government's cut to disability funding, which was subsequently reversed. The Cork journalist was born with the rare disability Total Amelia, but her motto has always been 'No limbs, no limits'. At just sixteen, she got a standing ovation when she addressed the United Nations in New York.

18th February 1939

Estella Solomons organised a Dublin exhibition for artists fleeing Europe before World War II. Born into a prominent Jewish family, Estella was a leading artist of her generation. She was a member of her local Cumann na mBan, and her studio was used as a safe house by volunteers. A number of her painted portraits of republican leaders had to be destroyed to avoid incriminating them.

19th February 1900

Alice Milligan's play *The Last Feast of the Fianna* opened at Dublin's Gaiety Theatre for a week-long run. The Tyrone woman was prolific, producing plays, poetry, novels, short stories and articles. She was a leading political figure and co-founder of *The Shan Van Vocht* nationalist journal. Admired for her energy and determination, she was once described as 'a darling little electric battery'.

20th February 1985

The government finally voted to allow the sale of contraceptives without prescription. Limited access had been introduced in 1980, for 'bona fide family planning' only. The Catholic Church fought hard against the 1985 bill, forecasting a 'slippery slope of moral degradation'. In the end, there were just three votes between the ayes and the nays.

21st February 1872

Anna Haslam and her husband founded the committee that would become the Dublin Women's Suffrage Association. Anna was secretary of the DWSA for nearly three decades and never missed a single meeting. As a young woman, she volunteered in Famine soup kitchens and set up lace-making and knitting cottage industries for local women. When women over thirty finally got the vote in 1918, ninety-year-old Anna was greeted with cheers and flowers at her local voting station.

22nd February 1996

The documentary *Dear Daughter* was first broadcast on RTÉ, detailing the systematic abuse Christine Buckley suffered in her thirteen years in Goldenbridge orphanage. Christine's revelations helped to break the silence around conditions in religious institutions and kickstarted a nationwide discussion. She set up the Aislinn Centre (now the Christine Buckley Centre) and was a tireless and inspiring advocate for survivors.

23rd February 1929

Impressive all-rounder Norma Stoker earned her first international hockey cap. Born and raised in Dublin,

Norma made her career at the French embassy. But in her spare time, she was goalie for the Irish hockey team, won two Irish tennis doubles titles, and represented her country in badminton. In her later years, she took up golf and croquet and, not unexpectedly, excelled in both.

24th February 2022

Dr Karen Weekes arrived in Barbados after rowing three thousand miles across the Atlantic Ocean. She was the first Irish woman to make the journey solo. The Galway sports psychologist spent eighty days in her twenty-five-foot boat, getting just four hours' sleep a night. No stranger to endurance sports, Karen has also circumnavigated Ireland in a kayak, climbed Kilimanjaro and cycled solo across Canada.

25th February 1904

Máire Ní Chinnéide was appointed the first president of the Camogie Association. After standing on the sidelines of men's hurling for years, Máire led the group of women who drew up the rules for camogie. In the very first public camogie match, she scored the first goal – ankle-length skirt and all. Also an Irish-language activist, Máire translated *Grimms' Fairy Tales* and edited Peig Sayers's iconic autobiography.

26th February 2021

The Consul General of Ireland in L.A. hosted a special event called 'Women & the Director's Chair' celebrating a trio of award-winning Irish directors. Emmy winner Dearbhla Walsh has worked on TV dramas like *Bad Sisters*, Lisa Mulcahy has two IFTAs for her film and TV work, and Neasa Hardiman was a BAFTA winner for *Happy Valley*. Their work reflects the surge in female directing talent in Ireland.

27th February 1841

A poem by Frances Browne was published in *The Irish*

Penny Journal. The Donegal woman had become blind after catching smallpox at the age of eighteen months. But she was a prodigy, composing her first poem at the tender age of seven. She overcame blindness and poverty to forge a career as a writer in Edinburgh and London, garnering the nickname 'the Blind Poetess of Ulster'.

28th February 1938

Alice Taylor was born on a farm in County Cork. She later moved to the village of Innishannon, running the local shop and post office. Her life was to change dramatically when her memoir *To School Through the Fields* was published in 1988. It became one of Ireland's bestselling books ever. Since then, she has written much-loved memoirs, poetry, novels, and even a children's book, with her daughter. Always mindful of those who have gone before us, Alice believes, 'We walk in the footprints of great women.'

MARCH

1st March 1976

The first issue of feminist newspaper *Banshee* was published by Irishwomen United. With strong views on contraception and abortion, it was fiercely critical of the Catholic Church. Its British counterpart, *Spare Rib*, was banned as obscene here the following year, sparking a protest march on International Women's Day.

2nd March 2024

Inspirational activist Sarah Grace appeared on *The Tommy Tiernan Show*. She shocked viewers with details of how survivors of sexual violence are treated by Ireland's archaic justice system – including being forced to hand over private therapy notes and testifying within touching distance of their attackers. The French-Irish lawyer has drawn on her experience as a survivor to campaign for immediate and radical changes to court processes.

3rd March 2020

Architects Yvonne Farrell and Shelley McNamara were the very first Irish recipients of the Pritzker Prize, their industry's highest award. The two women founded Grafton Architects in 1978 and grew a reputation for sophisticated, bold designs, including Università Luigi Bocconi in Milan, which bagged them the World Building of the Year Award.

4th March 2021

Limerick hip-hop artist Denise Chaila won the Choice Music Prize for her album *Go Bravely*. Denise moved to Ireland from Zambia with her family as a child. She released her debut EP *Duel Citizenship* in 2019. She says, 'I'm good at my job, it's something I love, and I do it to a standard of excellence. Within that I represent womanhood.'

5th **March** 2019

A portrait of Dr Victoria 'Vicki' Coffey was unveiled
at the Royal College of Surgeons. The Dublin doctor
was one of our first women paediatricians, qualifying in
1943. Vicki lost a brother and sister when she was just
eleven years old, which may well have influenced her
career choice. She specialised in congenital birth defects
and Sudden Infant Death Syndrome (SIDS), both
understudied areas at the time.

6th **March** 1971

Two founding members of the Irish Women's
Liberation Movement appeared on *The Late Late
Show* and kicked off *quite* the heated debate. Nell
McCafferty and Máirín Johnston were launching the
group's manifesto, 'Chains or Change'. Their demands
included equal pay, equal education and freely available
contraception. Though a short-lived movement, the
IWLM was radical and influential. Its members would

go on to found Irish Women's Aid, the Rape Crisis
Centre and the National Women's Council.

7th March 1985

Sr Stanislaus 'Stan' Kennedy founded Focus Ireland,
now Ireland's largest voluntary organisation for the
homeless. The charismatic Kerrywoman always had an
unshakable belief in a fairer society. She also founded
the Immigrant Council of Ireland, which has helped
tens of thousands of migrants. In a 2014 poll, Sr Stan
was voted Ireland's Greatest Woman.

8th March 2023

A sculpture of Kate Kennedy was unveiled in her
hometown of Duleek, County Meath. Kate had
emigrated to the US with her family during the
Famine. She trained as a teacher and was quickly
promoted to principal. But when she learned she was
to be paid substantially less than her male counterparts,

she didn't take it lying down. She was the first woman in the world to win a legal action for equal pay.

9th March 1926

Margaret Buckley first represented Dublin at the Sinn Féin Ard Fheis. She would go on to become president of the party a decade later, the first female leader of any Irish political party. She was deeply critical of the 1937 constitution and of 'De Valera's treating the women of this country as half-wits'. On the day it came into force, she flew a black flag in protest.

10th March 2021

A new TG4 documentary on Peig Sayers took a fresh look at the legendary Kerry storyteller. Peig moved to the Great Blasket Island when she married and lived there for fifty years. She became best known for her 1936 memoir, *Peig, a Scéal Féin* (*Peig, Her Own Story*), though it would be much maligned by eye-rolling teenagers. Long before Madonna and Beyoncé, she was a woman immediately recognisable by just her first name.

11th March 1925

The Children's Sunshine Home in Stillorgan, which cared for children with life-limiting conditions, was co-founded by Letitia Overend and Dr Ella Webb. Letitia was a lifetime member of St. John Ambulance and had nursed the wounded from both sides during the Rising. A huge fan of motor cars, she was nicknamed 'Miss Rolls Royce'. Gardaí were said to turn a blind eye to her shockingly haphazard parking.

12th March 1885

Sophie Bryant was the first woman published by the London Mathematical Society. Sophie had moved from Dublin to London as a teenager and started a degree as soon as women were allowed. She was the first British or Irish woman to become a Doctor of Science, and the first woman to publish a maths textbook. (But let's not hold that against her.)

13th March 2006

Twenty-four-year-old Derval O'Rourke arrived back in Dublin brandishing her World Championship gold medal for the 60m hurdles. She also snagged herself silver in the 100m hurdles in the 2006 and 2010 European Championships. Ireland had a long tradition over middle and long distance, but the Corkonian put us on the map for hurdles as well.

14th March 1991

When the Birmingham Six were finally freed, Paddy Hill gave special thanks to Sr Sarah Clarke, who he called the 'Joan of Arc' of British prisons. Sarah came from Galway but later moved to England. She became involved in the Northern Ireland civil rights movement, particularly the treatment of republican prisoners. When the Guildford Four were freed, Paul Hill would only pose for a newspaper photo with Sarah by his side.

15th March 1745

Dublin's Rotunda Hospital was founded on this day. The first maternity hospital in the then British Empire, it opened with ten beds and the most basic equipment. Judith Rochford was the first woman to give birth there. Within a year, 208 babies had been delivered, though only 109 survived. The Rotunda is the oldest continuously operating maternity hospital in the world.

16th March 1936

Teresa Deevy's best-known play, *Katie Roche*, opened at the Abbey Theatre. Teresa was born in Waterford and became deaf at the age of nineteen due to illness. She began writing in her twenties, often intricate plays exploring women's role in society. Her open criticism of censorship and the Catholic Church meant that she eventually fell out of favour at the Abbey. Her work has been rightfully rediscovered in recent years.

17th March 2013

The Irish women's rugby team clinched its first Six Nations Grand Slam with a victory over Italy in Milan. In freezing conditions, Fiona Coghlan's team went behind but rallied to secure the win. Earlier in the campaign, Ireland beat England for the first time, with a superb score of 25-0. Something for the men's team to aim for.

18th March 1955

Ruby Murray was the first artist ever to have five songs in the UK Top 20 at the same time. Belfast-born Ruby had a throat operation as a child which gave her a distinctively husky singing voice. She was spotted in London by a talent scout for Columbia Records and signed right away. She was so popular through the 1950s that her name even became Cockney rhyming slang – for 'curry'. #madeit

19th March 1954

The Irish Countrywomen's Association took over An Grianán in Termonfeckin, County Louth. It became the country's first residential centre for adult education. Founded in 1910, the ICA is Ireland's largest women's organisation. Though many of us think the 'country' in ICA means rural, it actually means Ireland – the ICA's biggest guild is in bustling Blanchardstown.

20th March 1969

The Irish Family Planning Association was officially founded. It opened Ireland's first family planning clinic in Merrion Square, Dublin. At the time, the only legal contraceptive that could be prescribed to women was the pill. Condoms or diaphragms had to be posted from Donegal by Northern Irish doctors – or smuggled through customs by the elderly mother and mother-in-law of one of the doctors.

21ˢᵗ March 1970

Dana Rosemary Scallon won the Eurovision Song Contest, held in Amsterdam. Ireland's first ever winner, she was just eighteen years of age. Her sweet and wholesome 'All Kinds of Everything' sold two million copies globally and launched a decades-long career. Not content with her music success, the original Derry girl also went on to become an MEP for Connacht-Ulster. Douze points.

22ⁿᵈ March 1890

Mary Lee had the first of her compelling 'Letters to Women' published in an Australian newspaper. After emigrating from Monaghan to care for her adult son, Mary became heavily involved with the women's movement. She co-founded the South Australian Women's Suffrage League in 1888. Just six years later, women in the state got the vote and were also entitled to stand for parliament – a world first.

23rd March 2018

Professor Margaret Murnane was awarded a Science Foundation of Ireland medal in Washington, DC. The Limerick woman has designed some of the world's fastest lasers, which pulse at trillionths of a second. For her outstanding research, she was the second woman ever to win the Boyle Medal. Margaret relishes being an educator and a role model – she was in grad school before she met her first female physics lecturer.

24th March 1826

Belfast's Poor House Ladies Committee was officially co-founded by Mary Ann McCracken. Its mission was to educate disadvantaged children and find them apprenticeships. Mary Ann spent her life fighting for social reform. In her late eighties, she was still handing out anti-slavery leaflets. She firmly lived up to her motto: 'It's better to wear out than rust out.'

25th March 1964

The Guardianship of Infants Act was signed into law, giving both parents joint guardianship over their children. Before this date, married fathers chose their children's religious education, giving them an advantage in custody cases. Newsflash: Women finally secure joint legal rights to the children they physically gave birth to.

26th March 1990

Brenda Fricker was the first Irish woman to win an acting Oscar, for her portrayal of Christy Brown's mother, Bridget, in the acclaimed film *My Left Foot*. The Dubliner's stage and screen career has spanned several decades, but she still has a down-to-earth approach to life – she famously claimed that her Oscar statuette held her bathroom door open. She dedicated the award to Bridget Fagan-Brown, saying that anyone who gave birth twenty-two times deserved an Oscar.

27th March 1999

B*Witched topped the UK charts with the ever-so-catchy 'Blame It on the Weatherman'. The Dublin quartet were the first group to have their first four singles hit No. 1. After their time in the limelight, the jigging popsters had sold over three million albums – and done wonders for double denim.

28th March 2023

Figures showed that Ireland had increased its representation of women in parliament to just 23.1%. That's lower than the parliaments of Iraq and South Sudan, neither of which is renowned for its progressive attitude to women. Gender quotas introduced for the 2016 General Election here resulted in a 6.5% increase in seats held by women.

29th March 1978

The Rutland Centre for addiction treatment was co-founded by Mary Bolton. Mary overcame her own addiction and became widely respected for her psychotherapy methods. More than ten thousand people have been treated at the Rutland for addiction to food, drugs, sex, gaming, porn and gambling. Mary also founded Narcotics Anonymous in Ireland in 1983. Her life impacted countless others.

30th March 1778

Lady Eleanor Butler and Sarah Ponsonby escaped from Ireland across the Irish Sea. Eleanor, then forty years old, feared she was to be placed in a convent by her family. Sarah faced the prospect of a marriage she didn't want. Following their escape, the two set up home in Wales and became known as the Ladies of Llangollen. They lived together for the rest of their lives and were buried beside each other in the local graveyard.

31st March 1981

Kildare-born make-up artist Michele Burke won her first Oscar for her work on *Quest for Fire*. She won her second for *Bram Stoker's Dracula* a decade later. Michele emigrated to Canada in the 1970s, working on iconic films with some of the acting greats. On her first Oscar nomination, she said, 'I put the phone down and never thought twice about it at the time because I didn't know what it meant.' She was a little less blasé about it the second time around.

APRIL

1st **April** 2022

Dr Orla Flynn was appointed the first president of the newly merged Atlantic Technological University. She joined other women presidents of Trinity, University of Limerick, Maynooth, South East Tech and Munster Tech. In 2019, there were no women presidents of Irish universities. By 2022, there were six.

2nd **April** 1914

The Irish republican organisation Cumann na mBan was founded in Wynn's Hotel, Dublin. Meaning 'Women's Council', its founding members included Countess Markievicz, Kathleen Clarke and Mary MacSwiney. Active throughout the War of Independence, members smuggled and stored arms, carried dispatches and gathered intelligence. Its role in historical events has long been undervalued.

3rd April 1993

The new Criminal Justice Act was signed into law, allowing victim impact statements in court and the review of unduly lenient sentences. These momentous steps were a result of the campaign by Kilkenny woman Lavinia Kerwick, the first Irish rape survivor to waive her right to anonymity. She was just nineteen years old at the time. Since then, more and more survivors have shown the same incredible strength in going public with their stories.

4th April 1922

Máire Mhac an tSaoi was born in Dublin, the same year the Irish state was founded. As a young woman, she studied languages and joined the diplomatic service. On her posting to the embassy in Madrid, she began writing Irish poetry. Her body of work includes numerous poetry collections and the award-winning novel *A Bhean Óg Ón*. She is credited with helping to reinvigorate Irish language literature.

5th April 1964

Eileen Kennedy became Ireland's first female judge. She was assigned to the Children's Court in Dublin. From Carrickmacross, County Monaghan, she was known for her fairness and compassion. She was strongly in favour of replacing reformatory schools with foster care and increasing the age of criminal responsibility from seven to twelve – which wouldn't happen until more than twenty years after her death.

6th April 1899

A new law meant that Irish women could vote in local elections for the first time. They could also stand for district councils. Thirty-five women were elected to rural and urban councils. It would be another twenty years before (some) women would vote in national elections.

7th April 1951

The Central Remedial Clinic was co-founded by Lady Valerie Goulding and Kathleen O'Rourke to care for children with polio. It is now the country's largest organisation for people with disabilities. Valerie had moved to Ireland from Kent and was shocked by the poverty here. After setting up the CRC, she oversaw its operation until 1984. She was once described as 'part Thatcher, part Florence Nightingale, and part sergeant-major'.

8th April 1990

Fiona Shaw scooped the Olivier Award for a trio of outstanding stage performances in London. The much-loved Cork actor trained at RADA and honed her skills at the Royal Shakespeare Company. Her roles have spanned award-winning theatre, film and TV, including hit shows like *True Blood* and *Killing Eve*. Trained as a classical singer, she has a wonderfully distinctive speaking voice. You'd listen to her narrate the phonebook.

9th **April** 1924

Cynthia Longfield boarded the *St George* for an expedition to the Pacific Islands. It would be an eighteen-month, 300,000-mile trip to study beetles, butterflies and moths (oh my!). The Cork woman was an adventurer at heart and well able to hack her way through the jungle with a machete. She discovered several new insects and has two dragonfly species named after her. Her pioneering work earned her the nickname 'Madame Dragonfly'.

10th **April** 2021

Rachael Blackmore was first past the post at the Grand National at Aintree. The Tipperary native was the first woman champion in 182 years of the race. After a successful amateur career, Rachael has gone on to become one of the leading National Hunt jockeys. 'It was an honour to be the first woman to win the Grand National … I just felt elated that I had won, not elated because I was a female who had won.'

11th **April** 2021

Dublin footballer Katie McCabe earned her fiftieth international cap. The versatile player has won two league cups and an FA Cup with her club, Arsenal. She made her Ireland debut in 2015 and was our youngest-ever captain two years later. She scored our very first goal in a Women's World Cup in 2023, when she found the net direct from a corner kick. Get in!

12th **April** 1898

Nellie Cashman arrived in Dawson City in the Yukon, Canada, as a gold prospector. She was one of the few women to work her own claims. Originally from County Cork, Nellie emigrated to the US during the Famine. A formidable woman with a kind heart, she once led an eighty-day rescue mission to free trapped miners in British Columbia. It earned her the nickname 'the Miners' Angel'. She had no interest in marriage, saying, 'I prefer being pals with men to being cook for one man.'

13th April 1949

Carmel Snow was awarded the Legion of Honour for her service to the French fashion industry. The Dalkey native was *Harper's Bazaar*'s editor-in-chief in New York for more than two decades. She was known to have an iron will. When told not to include African Americans in the magazine, she went ahead and featured singer Marian Anderson. She defied her boss, the ferocious William Randolph Hearst, again and again. He eventually sent out a memo: 'Does anyone have any control over Mrs. Snow? I KNOW I don't.'

14th April 1995

A commemorative plaque for Cecil Frances Alexander was unveiled in Derry. The Dublin-born poet lived in the 1800s and showed a real flair for writing hymns. Her best known are 'Once in Royal David's City', 'There Is a Green Hill Far Away' and 'All Things Bright and Beautiful'. Packing them into the pews.

15th April 1900

Maud Gonne founded Ireland's first women's nationalist organisation, Inghínidhe na hÉireann (Daughters of Ireland). It offered classes in the Irish language and Irish history, music and art, and promoted Irish manufacturers. Born into a wealthy family, Maud was won over to the republican cause when she witnessed firsthand the viciousness of evictions. For a time, the Dublin slang 'maudgonning' meant agitating for a cause with recklessness and flamboyance.

16th **April** 2003

The film adaptation of Marian Keyes's first novel, *Watermelon*, was broadcast. Marian has been hugely successful, with a rake of bestsellers to her name. Readers are drawn to her humorous treatment of darker themes like addiction, depression and domestic violence. With stories centred on women characters, her writing is often classed as 'chick lit' – but Marian has rightly objected that there's no equivalent 'dick lit'.

17th **April** 1973

Mary Tinney was the only woman to attend a strategic conference on Ireland's foreign policy. Later that year, she was the first woman to be appointed an Irish ambassador. She had begun her diplomatic career in London, then Stockholm, where she danced a jig for Sweden's king. Her riverdancing did her no harm at all, as she went on to become ambassador to Sweden – then Belgium and Kenya.

18th **April** 2020

Dolores O'Riordan and the Cranberries hit one billion views for 'Zombie' on YouTube. The Limerick singer-songwriter started in her local church choir before leaving school to join the band. They sold 50 million albums worldwide, in no small part due to Dolores's lyrics and distinctive singing voice. Shortly after her untimely death in 2018, she was named 'Top Female Artist of All Time' on Billboard's Alternative Songs chart.

19th **April** 1963

The first issue of *Woman's Way* was published. It was the first Irish women's magazine to have a readers' letters page, which proved a big hit. Letters raised hot topic issues like women working outside the home, single mothers, contraception and family size. One Cork reader said it should be required reading for 'every priest, bishop and Dáil deputy in the country'.

20th April 2023

Dubliner Sinéad Burke made her second cover of British *Vogue*. In 2019, she had been the first little person to feature on their cover and the first to attend the prestigious Met Gala. Sinéad was born with achondroplasia and stands at three feet and five inches. Small but mighty, she is a powerhouse activist. She won acclaim for her TED talk 'Why Design Should Include Everyone' and her children's book *Break the Mould*.

21st April 1986

Mary Redmond founded the Irish Hospice Foundation. Born and raised in Dublin, Mary got her PhD in Law from Cambridge. She later returned to Ireland to care for her ill father and struggled to find a hospice place for him. She vowed that there would be more hospice beds – and she was true to her word. Her foundation would not only set up a second Dublin hospice but change attitudes to end-of-life care in Ireland.

22nd April 2020

CMAT launched her music career with her first single, 'Another Day (kfc)'. Reared in the Royal County, Ciara Mary-Alice Thompson 'always knew I was a pop star but nobody else believed me'. Her first two albums went straight to No. 1 on release. Her debut album, *If My Wife New I'd Be Dead,* won the Choice Music Prize. *Hot Press* called it 'one of the most thrilling Irish pop debuts of the century'.

23rd April 2019

Ailbhe Smyth was named one of *Time* magazine's 100 most influential people in the world, with her co-founders of Together for Yes. They led a grassroots movement to pass the 2018 abortion referendum. Ailbhe is a feminist academic and LGBTQ+ activist. Now in her seventies, there is lots more that she wants to achieve – including ensuring that older women aren't made invisible. Her attitude? 'Never give in, never give up.'

24ᵗʰ April 1916

Ahead of the Rising, the Proclamation of the Republic was signed in Jennie Wyse Power's restaurant on Henry Street. Jennie was a lynchpin of everything from Cumann na mBan to Daughters of Ireland to Sinn Féin. When elected to Dublin Corporation in 1920, she signed her name *as Gaeilge*. When that disqualified her, she gave the clerk hell. Kathleen Clarke said, 'She was an extremely clever woman and well able to defend herself … I never admired any woman as I did her that day.' The clerk (wisely) backed down.

25ᵗʰ April 2018

Vicky Phelan settled her High Court action against a US laboratory. She had been diagnosed with advanced cervical cancer after an incorrect smear test result. She refused to sign a non-disclosure agreement, instead heroically campaigning for immediate changes to Ireland's screening service. She also called for the introduction of the HPV vaccine in secondary schools. Vicky tragically passed away in November 2022, aged just forty-eight.

26ᵗʰ April 1916

Margaret Skinnider was shot three times during the Rising and was unable to make it to a hospital for three days. Born in Scotland to Irish parents, she had trained as a teacher. When she heard of the imminent rebellion, she left her job in Glasgow and came to Ireland, smuggling bomb detonators on her way. She was a scout and sniper and the only woman wounded in action. Because of her gender, she wasn't granted a military pension until 1938.

27ᵗʰ April 1920

Georgina 'Georgie' Frost became the first woman in Ireland or Britain to hold a position in the law courts. The Lord Lieutenant of Ireland had decided that a woman was not 'a proper person' for a job as a petty sessions clerk in County Clare. Georgie sued and lost. Unbowed, she appealed to the House of Lords and won.

28th April 1952

Longford woman Eleanor Whitton organised a meeting in Dublin to highlight the issue of animal welfare. A month earlier, she had led a thousand-strong protest through the city. Eleanor was a one-woman army who fought to improve the conditions of horses being exported, and ultimately to ban live export altogether. With the courage of her convictions, she personally bought thousands of horses to rescue them.

29th April 1965

Dublin driver Rosemary Smith won the Netherlands' Tulip Rally – the only woman ever to win it. Having originally trained as a dress designer, she more than held her own in a sport dominated by men. Once, during the London to Sydney rally, a mechanical failure brought her to a stop. 'I remember my father saying to me that if a car wouldn't go forward, it would usually go in reverse. So I reversed for 53km up the Khyber Pass.'

30ᵗʰ April 1813

Acclaimed writer Maria Edgeworth arrived in London at the pinnacle of her career and was welcomed as a literary lion. She had been an immediate success from her debut novel, *Castle Rackrent,* and included Jane Austen among her fans. She used her book royalties to buy the family's Longford estate from her brother – but allowed him to keep up the pretence that he was still in charge. During the Famine, aged eighty, she went door to door distributing food to neighbours.

MAY

1st May 1967

A new type of diamond was named for Kildare-born crystallographer Kathleen Lonsdale. Kathleen studied physics and was University College London's first female professor. During World War II she spent a month in prison as a conscientious objector – this inspired her to campaign for better prison conditions. The diamond that carries her name, lonsdaleite, is thought to be 50% tougher than regular diamond. Seems fitting.

2nd May 1980

Joan Doran became Dublin Bus's first woman bus driver. The Ballyfermot woman was the first on a scheduled run here since before World War II. By 2016, Dublin Bus had its first ever all-women graduating class. Their 'More Mná' campaign aims to recruit even more widely. Let's not forget: statistically safer drivers.

3rd May 1757

Peg Woffington made her final stage appearance in Covent Garden. She was one of the finest actors of her day. Born into poverty in Dublin, Peg started as a child performer in a tightrope show. Her first major acting role was as Ophelia in *Hamlet*, but she had a particular flair for 'breeches' roles (where she played a man). She split her time between Dublin and London, with Smock Alley luring her back to Dublin for a record salary.

4th May 1925

Twenty-two-year-old Dubliner Oonah Keogh lodged her application to become the world's first woman stockbroker, decades ahead of her New York and London counterparts. Approval of Oonah's application owed a lot to Ireland's brand-new constitution of equality – she could not be denied simply because she was a woman. She went on to sell, sell, sell for fourteen years.

5th May 1941

Limerick-born Kate O'Brien's *The Land of Spices* was banned by the censor. The resulting outrage would lead to the setting up of an appeals procedure. Kate's novels often drew on controversial themes of female agency and sexuality, and they included queer characters. She was once asked in a letter from a mother superior why her novels were so scandalous. Kate answered by telegram: 'Pounds, shillings and pence.'

6th May 1908

Dublin-born suffragist Mary Maloney repeatedly disrupted a Winston Churchill speech in Dundee, Scotland, by ringing a bell. Demanding an apology for insulting remarks he made about women's suffrage, she and her bell followed him around for a week. Later that year, Mary and four other suffragists climbed the Coeur de Lion statue outside Westminster. She was arrested but had her £5 fine paid by a friend – 'much to her chagrin'.

7th May 2007

Easkey Britton became the first woman to surf the big wave called Aill na Searrach. Meaning 'Leap of the Foals', this wave can reach a massive height of thirty-five feet before breaking beneath the Cliffs of Moher. Easkey was born in Donegal and learned to surf at the tender age of four. She won our national women's title five years in a row, as well as the British Pro-Tour championship. She was the first woman to surf off the coast of Iran.

8th May 1903

Skibbereen woman Agnes Clerke was made an honorary member of the Royal Astronomical Society, crowning a lifelong dedication to the study of the stars. She wrote widely on the subject. Her best-known book, *A Popular History of Astronomy during the Nineteenth Century*, is still in print 140 years later. She is one of two Irish women with moon craters named after them.

9th May 2022

It was announced that Mary Crilly would receive the Freedom of Cork City. At the ceremony the following month, poet Paula Meehan paid tribute to Mary's 'magnificent wildness'. She founded the Sexual Violence Centre Cork in 1983 and has helped thousands of survivors. In the centre's early years, Mary was treated with suspicion by some locals – even told she wasn't welcome in Cork. More recently she has been given the plaudits she deserves.

10th May 1916

The iconic photograph of Patrick Pearse surrendering after the Rising was first published on the front page of the *London Daily Sketch*. The skirts and feet of Elizabeth O'Farrell had been airbrushed out of it – for some, a symbol of women being erased from history. A dedicated republican and trained nurse, Elizabeth tended to the wounded in Moore Street during the

Rising and carried the message of surrender to the British. She was there at the surrender, but when she saw a soldier getting ready to take a photo, she stepped back behind Pearse. She always regretted it.

11th May 1974

The founders of Women's Aid gave their first press conference. Journalist Maureen Fox and politician Nuala Fennell had read reports of women moving to the UK with their children to escape abusive partners. A couple of months later, Women's Aid opened its first refuge on Harcourt Street. Today, it is one of the country's leading organisations tackling domestic violence.

12th May 1709

Susanna Centlivre's restoration comedy *The Busie Body* opened in London's Drury Lane. She was the first Irish woman to have international success as a playwright. As a teenager, Susanna had run away from her Tyrone home, dressing as a boy to attend lectures in Cambridge. She became an actor and started writing plays, often with smart, articulate women characters. She found the widespread prejudice against female playwrights frustrating: 'Since the Poet is born, why not a Woman as well as a Man?'

13th May 1919

One of the earliest surviving issues of the radical journal on sexual politics, *Urania*, was published by Eva Gore-Booth and trans woman Irene Clyde. Its editorial called for 'the abolition of the "manly" and the "womanly". Will you not help to sweep them into the museum of antiques?' Eva and her older sister, Constance (later Markievicz), lived a life of luxury growing up in Sligo, but both would become deeply involved in politics and social causes. Eva relocated to Manchester in her twenties to join her lifelong love, Esther Roper.

Together, the pair were strident trade unionists and suffragists. Devoted to one another, they are buried together, their grave bearing a Sappho quote.

14th May 2023

Sharon Horgan's whip-smart black comedy *Bad Sisters* won the BAFTA for Best Drama. She co-wrote and starred as one of five sisters plotting to bump off a supremely nasty husband. Sharon had previously shown form with crowd-pleasers *Pulling*, *Motherland* and *Catastrophe*. She loves writing funny women: 'I think that's important in comedy, that we get a lot of the good lines and you're not just the girlfriend or the sister.' Amen.

15th May 1939

Maureen O'Hara's major film debut, *Jamaica Inn*, made her Ireland's first A-list actor. Maureen grew up in Ranelagh, Dublin, and was just seventeen when she signed her first studio contract. She starred in over fifty films, including classics *The Quiet Man* and *Miracle on 34th Street*. Her characters were often known for their gumption. In real life, she was outspoken about the sexual harassment that was rampant in Hollywood.

16th May 1922

Eileen Gray opened her showroom in Paris. Self-taught and minimalist, the Wexford woman was one of the most influential furniture designers of the 20th century. Her 'Dragons' armchair sold for a record-breaking €21.9 million in 2009. As an architect, her most famous building, E-1027, was an iconic villa on the French coast. Its contents included a combination of mirrors to show you the back of your head and a tea trolley with a cork surface (to stop the cups rattling).

17th May 1928

Lady Mary Heath landed in London after her solo flight from Cape Town. She descended from the plane dressed to the nines, including high heels, furs and pearls. Mary was the first woman pilot to perform a loop the loop and to parachute from a plane. She was also the UK's first female commercial pilot, though only after completing the physical tests while menstruating. Up until then, the aviation commission deemed the menstrual cycle a disability that made women unfit.

18th May 1998

Aran Islander Bridget Dirrane was the oldest person in the world to be awarded a degree when NUI Galway honoured the 103-year-old for a full and varied life. Bridget had been a member of Cumann na mBan who discussed plans with the 1916 leaders. When living in the US, she was an Air Force nurse and canvassed for JFK. She spent her final decades back on Inis Mór.

19th May 1772

A eulogy for Cork woman Elizabeth Aldworth appeared in the *Public Gazetteer*. Elizabeth's father was a master freemason. As a teenager, she accidentally overheard one of his meetings and to avoid the obligatory death penalty for eavesdropping, he had her sworn in as the first woman freemason. She fully embraced it, often turning up at events wearing full masonic regalia.

20th May 1909

A benefit concert was held in Dublin for soprano Margaret Burke Sheridan to raise the £600 she needed to attend London's Royal Academy of Music. It would set her on the road to stardom. After London, she trained in Rome, then debuted in Puccini's *La Bohème*. She played all the leading Italian opera houses and became known as 'La Sheridan'. She preferred to call herself 'Maggie from Mayo'.

21st May 1907

Irish mountaineer Elizabeth Hawkins-Whitshed founded the Ladies' Alpine Club. She was later known as the impossibly cool Lizzie Le Blond. Raised in Wicklow, she was captivated by mountaineering and photography. Always with her trusty camera to hand, she was the first person to photograph dozens of ascents across the Alps and the Norwegian Arctic. After her first climb, her grand-aunt sent an SOS to Lizzie's mother: 'Stop her climbing mountains! She is scandalising all London.'

22nd May 1971

Members of the Irish Women's Liberation Movement took the 'Contraceptive Train' from Dublin to Belfast to protest Ireland's outdated laws on birth control. In Belfast, they bought as much spermicidal jelly and condoms as they could carry. Without prescriptions, they bought aspirin instead of the pill, betting that customs officials wouldn't know the difference. There was huge media coverage of their triumphant return to Dublin, waving aloft their contraband.

23rd May 1706

When a British soldier was wounded at the Battle of Ramillies, 'he' was discovered to be a woman. Dubliner Christian 'Kit' Cavanagh joined the army after her husband was drafted. She distinguished herself as a soldier and was eventually reunited with him. When her gender was discovered, the army kept her on as a cook on full pay. On her death, she was given a military burial.

24th May 1785

George Anne Bellamy made her last stage appearance in London's Drury Lane. The Fingal-born actor had played a range of roles since her debut at ten years old. She was particularly popular in tragic romantic roles like Desdemona in *Othello* and Cordelia in *King*

Lear. In the Battle of the Romeos in 1750, with two simultaneous productions in Covent Garden and Drury Lane, she was widely considered the winning Juliet.

25th May 2018

The referendum on repeal of the Eighth Amendment took place. The amendment made the life of a pregnant mother and the foetus she was carrying equal under Irish law. It had a disastrous effect on the medical care provided to women here and forced hundreds of thousands of women to travel to Britain for abortions. The referendum on introducing restricted abortion in Ireland was passed with a resounding two-thirds majority.

26th May 1989

It was the end of an era with the closing of Parsons Bookshop on Dublin's Baggot Street. The literary landmark had been opened forty years earlier by

Corkonian May O'Flaherty and run by a team of women. It was a popular haunt for Irish writers like Kavanagh and Behan, and later Binchy and Heaney. Mary Lavin said, 'One met as many interesting writers on the floor of the shop as on the shelves.'

27th May 1878

The Matrimonial Causes Act was passed, finally allowing women to leave their abusive husbands. It followed the publication of a powerful pamphlet on 'wife torture' by Dublin-born social reformer Frances Power Cobbe. She argued that 'the notion that a man's wife is his property, in the sense in which a horse is his property, is the fatal root of incalculable evil and misery'.

28th May 1940

When Germany invaded Belgium, teacher Mary O'Kelly de Galway joined the resistance there, smuggling weapons and translating strategic documents until she was arrested by the Gestapo. She spent the rest of the war in concentration camps and weighed just four stone when she was liberated. She received commendations from both Belgium and the US. In later life, Mary lived in Clontarf, where she was a popular local character.

29th May 1888

The pinnacle of Ada Rehan's acting career came with the opening of *The Taming of the Shrew* in London's Leicester Square. Born in Limerick, with fair skin and dark hair, she became known for her Celtic beauty. She began her career with a series of small roles in the US. At twenty-two, she was the lead performer on the New York stage and became one of its most beloved of the time.

30th May 1963

Ireland's first celebrity chef, Monica Sheridan, released

her debut cookbook. Her RTÉ show had made her a household name and introduced her audience to exotic dishes like pizza, pasta and quiche (ooh la la!). Totally unselfconscious in front of camera, she was known for her cheeky sense of humour. Rumour has it that the Irish Home Economics Teachers' Association made a formal complaint about how she licked her fingers while cooking.

31st May 1979

The groundbreaking RTÉ Radio programme *Women Today* was first broadcast. Presented by Marian Finucane, it was the first radio programme aimed at, presented and produced by women. That same year, Marian won the Prix Italia for a documentary following an Irish woman to England for an abortion. Marian went on to present the hugely popular *Liveline* and the *Marian Finucane Show*, earning her genuine legend status.

JUNE

1ˢᵗ **June** 1947

Joan Denise Moriarty's Cork Ballet Group had its debut performance. Told she was too tall to be a professional dancer, Joan set up her own ballet school in Mallow, County Cork. It was to be the first of many. She would go on to found Ireland's first professional ballet company and the Irish National Ballet. Her work introduced thousands of Irish children to dance.

2ⁿᵈ **June** 1955

Patricia Farrell placed an ad in *The Irish Times* seeking fellow parents of children with intellectual disabilities. She had been shocked that there was no school place for her son Brian, who had Down Syndrome. Her ad led to the founding of St. Michael's House. Starting with just three students in a house in Dublin, it now provides services to 1,500 people with disabilities.

3rd June 1944

Maureen Sweeney took weather readings through the night at Blacksod Lighthouse, County Mayo. Her report of an impending storm had a decisive effect on the outcome of World War II. The D-Day landings were postponed by twenty-four hours, saving many Allied soldiers' lives. Maureen's contribution to victory was commended by the US Congress in 2021.

4th June 2012

Visually impaired athlete Sinead Kane took part in the 2012 Dublin Women's Mini Marathon. She went on to be the first visually impaired person in Ireland to run an ultramarathon. Then the first in the world to complete seven marathons on seven continents in seven days. Sinead is a qualified lawyer with two PhDs who lectures on disability law and policy – she only began running as a hobby.

5th June 2018

Cavan golfer Leona Maguire turned professional. The year she turned twenty-one, she had had to forfeit €68,000 in prize money because she was still an amateur. Once a pro, she was the first Irish woman to win on the LPGA tour. She holds the lowest score in the final round of any major championship – man or woman – with a 61. Ten birdies and not a bogey in sight.

6th June 1968

A major retrospective exhibition of Mary Swanzy's work opened in the Hugh Lane Gallery. The Dublin-born artist was Ireland's first Cubist and is now widely recognised as a master. She tried her hand at portraits first but found men reluctant to be painted by a woman. She was keenly aware of the impact her gender had on her career: 'If I had been born Henry instead of Mary, my life would have been very different.'

7th **June** 1861

Mary O'Connell (Sr Anthony) travelled to Ohio's Camp Dennison to nurse wounded soldiers in the American Civil War. She had emigrated from Limerick as a child, later joining the Sisters of Charity. During the war, she developed the first battlefield triage, allowing faster treatment of the wounded and preventing amputations. She earned the nickname 'the Angel of the Battlefield', and it was widely known amongst soldiers and doctors that her word was THE LAW.

8th **June** 2019

The official launch of Flossie and the Beach Cleaners took place in Dun Laoghaire. Led by Flossie Donnelly, the group meets every week to clear plastic and rubbish from Irish beaches. Flossie started cleaning beaches when she was just nine years old. She also stages climate strikes and has been dubbed Ireland's Greta Thunberg.

9th June 1903

Trinity College announced that it would award degrees to women from the following year. With colleges in Britain yet to do the same, women travelled from Oxford and Cambridge to graduate here – in all, 720 of them over the following three years. They had passed their exams and would already have graduated if they were men. They became known as 'the Steamboat Ladies'.

10th June 1977

A new, green £1 note was launched featuring Queen Medb, the warrior queen of Connacht. Medb was best known (and vilified) for her role in the epic Táin Bó Cuailnge. She was first mentioned in an Ogham inscription in the Cave of Cruachan in the 4th or 5th century. She ruled for sixty years and tied the knot no less than five times.

11th June 2022

Boxer Kellie Harrington was awarded the Freedom of
Dublin City for her incredible sporting achievements.
Young Kellie wanted to join her local boxing club,
but it only trained boys. They took her on and even
partitioned off a changing room just for her. She went
on to win first silver and then gold in the World Boxing
Championships. And watched by the entire country,
she clinched gold at the Tokyo Olympics and again at
Paris 2024. Unforgettable scenes.

12th June 1983

The first Women's Mini-Marathon took place in
Dublin. Nine thousand runners and walkers took
part that first time, and the numbers have swelled up
to forty thousand in the years since. It is the biggest
single-day charity event in the country and has raised
hundreds of millions for Irish charities. All for a good
cause!

13th June 1912

A group of women including Hanna Sheehy-Skeffington were arrested for smashing windows in Dublin Castle. The stone-throwers were protesting that women's suffrage was not included in the Home Rule Bill. They served sentences of one to six months for wilful damage. Well-behaved women seldom make history.

14th June 1913

Grace Gifford's illustrations appeared in the *Irish Citizen* newspaper. A talented artist, she also designed costumes for the Abbey Theatre. Often recognised only for her marriage to 1916 leader Joseph Plunkett, Grace was a staunch republican in her own right. She was elected to the executive of Sinn Féin and, like many anti-Treaty activists, was arrested and detained in Kilmainham. She painted murals on the walls of her cell. When she died, she was given a funeral with full military honours.

15th **June** 2006

Five of Molly Keane's acclaimed novels were re-issued a decade after her death. Believing that women couldn't succeed as writers, she wrote her first eleven novels under the pen name M.J. Farrell. Later in her career, she launched back onto the literary scene with her black comedy *Good Behaviour*. It was published under her own name and shortlisted for the 1981 Booker Prize. Molly continued publishing novels well into her eighties.

16th **June** 1977

The general election saw twenty-six women candidates running for Dáil seats. The Women's Political Association ran a strong campaign with slogans 'Why not a woman?' and 'Who's your woman?' First-preference votes for women doubled on the previous election.

17th June 1981

A new law introduced protection orders and increased barring orders up to twelve months. Ireland's first domestic violence legislation had come into force five years before but needed strengthening. The 1981 law also abolished 'crim con' (criminal conversation, where 'conversation' was an ancient term for sex). Crim con meant that a husband could legally sue another man for compensation for sleeping with his wife. But never the other way around, naturally.

18th June 1730

Constantia Grierson was the first woman in Ireland and Britain appointed as the king's printer. She was born in Kilkenny and, unusually for a woman of the time, studied the Classics. She married a printer and edited many of his publications. His application to the king boasted that Constantia's meticulous editing brought his printing 'to greater Perfection than has been hitherto in this

Kingdom'. So impressed was the Lord Lieutenant that he coupled her name with her husband's for the patent.

19th June 1976

Mary Dunlop co-founded Irish Guide Dogs for the Blind with Jim Dennehy. Mary had learned of the restrictions blind people face from the experience of her uncle. She adopted and trained a German Shepherd, Jan, and they put on shows to fundraise. In the mid-1970s, people were still sceptical about the benefits of guide dogs. Nowadays, nearly four hundred Irish people use guide and assistance dogs.

20th June 1972

Aileen McCorkell and her husband welcomed the IRA and MI6 to their Derry home to negotiate a ceasefire. Born in India, Aileen spent her childhood in County Louth. When she moved to Derry, she set up a branch of the Red Cross. As the Troubles escalated, she was respected by both sides for treating everyone equally in what had become a war zone. When asked how to get a Red Cross vehicle through a hostile crowd, she said 'Put your head out the window and roar!'

21st June 2019

After more than thirty years, former garda Majella Moynihan received an apology from the Garda Commissioner. At the age of twenty-two, Majella was charged with misconduct for having a child out of wedlock. Faced with hostile misogyny, Majella felt she had no option but to give her son up for adoption. Her career with the Gardaí was effectively ended. The father of her child, also an unmarried garda, was fined £90.

22nd June 1984

Maureen Potter was given the Freedom of Dublin City. The Fairview entertainer measured under 5ft but was certainly larger than life. She was the Queen of Panto, from her first role at the age of ten to her last more than fifty years later. She had a great trick of memorising the names of birthday children in the audience, then reeling them off – her record was sixty-seven. When she met children after the show, she would drink milk as a good example (though with a nip of whiskey added).

23rd June 1749

Eliza Bennis made the first entry in her diary, which she would keep for the next thirty years. The Limerick woman helped set up the Methodist movement in Ireland, and her writing gives valuable insights into the daily lives of women at the time. Lost when she emigrated to the US, her diary was rediscovered in 1999.

24th June 2017

A stage version of Emma Donoghue's *Room* opened at the Abbey Theatre. The original novel was shortlisted for the Booker Prize and Emma's screenplay adaptation was nominated for an Oscar. Emma was born in Dublin and studied at UCD before getting a PhD at Cambridge. She was just twenty-three when her first novel, *Stir Fry,* was published, and she has written over a dozen more. She reflects, 'Looking back on it, I can see I'm a rather typical Irish author in that most of my characters are gabby.'

25th June 1892

Ballyragget-born Mabel Cahill won the women's US open singles, doubles and mixed doubles titles. This made her the first player (female or male) to scoop the 'triple crown' at a major tournament. Mabel was an amateur but treated each game like a pro; she was renowned for her powerful groundstrokes. She is the only Irish player in the International Tennis Hall of Fame.

26th June 1997

Mary Harney became the first female Tánaiste in the

history of the state. The Galway native was the first woman to lead a modern political party here when she took over the Progressive Democrats. She once commented on gender difference in Leinster House, 'I never heard many men worry about the fact they didn't see their children … but I constantly heard women feeling guilty about their children.'

27th June 1939

Kathleen Clarke became Dublin's first woman mayor. It was then Ireland's highest-earning political position, with a whopping £2,500 salary. A lifelong republican, Kathleen had been a founder member of Cumann na mBan. As a TD and senator, she fought for single mothers' rights and raising the age of consent in sexual assault cases. Her first act as Lord Mayor was to refuse to wear the ceremonial chain as it bore the profile of William of Orange.

28th June 2020

Eileen Flynn was appointed a senator, the first Traveller to serve in the Oireachtas. A community activist for years, she grew up on the Labre Park halting site in Ballyfermot. She and her sister were the first members of their community to go to college. She is dedicated to challenging discrimination: 'If you can change one person's mind, they'll change another.'

29th June 2020

The Green Party's Hazel Chu was elected Lord Mayor of Dublin. She was the first person of Chinese heritage to hold the role (and the first to become mayor of a European capital). Hazel is outspoken on the need for more women in public office. 'Ask a guy to run, they generally respond with enthusiasm, whereas a woman is usually surprised at being asked.' We need to show girls and young women that they're more than capable.

30th June 1992

Siobhán Parkinson's first children's book, *The Dublin Adventure*, was published. She would go on to write more than two dozen books for children and teenagers. Siobhán was Ireland's first Laureate na nÓg / Children's Laureate. She founded Little Island children's publisher and still works in editing. Siobhán is visually impaired but uses electronic devices and audiobooks to do her work.

JULY

1st July 1956

Elizabeth Bowen had one of a series of articles published in US *Vogue*. The Dubliner's writing included short stories and novels on the Irish 'Big House', wartime London and ghost stories. Known to many as the grande dame of the modern novel, her best known were *The Death of the Heart* and *The Heat of the Day*. As a writer, she was interested in 'life with the lid on and what happens when the lid comes off'.

2nd July 1957

Bridie Gallagher topped the Irish charts with 'The Boys from the County Armagh', which went on to sell more than a quarter of a million copies. Bridie's career spanned five decades and saw her play everywhere from the Sydney Opera House to Carnegie Hall in New York. The girl from Donegal still holds the record for the largest audience in London's Albert Hall – now securely unbreakable due to modern health & safety.

3rd July 1911

Nationalist Helena Molony was arrested for throwing stones at a portrait of King George V ahead of his visit to Ireland. Her imprisonment made her the first female political prisoner in a generation. Helena was a magazine editor, trade unionist and actor. She used to come off stage at the Abbey Theatre, address nationalist meetings, and be back on stage before her next cue. She slept with copies of the Proclamation under her pillow – and a gun.

4th July 1890

Lena Rice won the Wimbledon ladies' singles title. The Tipperary woman earned twenty guineas and invented the forearm smash along the way – all while wearing the typical women's sporting attire of an ankle-length skirt, a blouse cinched at the waist, leather shoes and a straw hat. Today, the New Inn Tennis Club in Tipperary holds an annual competition in Lena's name.

5th July 1970

Margaret Hobbs took part in breaking the Falls Road Curfew. After a gun battle between British soldiers and the IRA, soldiers sealed off an area covering three thousand homes and carried out house-to-house searches. Thirty-six hours into the curfew, thousands of women and children marched into the area with food and supplies for locals. Margaret went on to become a renowned barrister and civil rights activist. She was a powerful advocate for survivors of domestic violence and sexual assault.

6th July 1881

Seventeen-year-old Offaly girl Kate Shelley saved the lives of two hundred people in her adopted home of Boone County, Iowa. In the midst of a terrible storm, a bridge over the Des Moines River collapsed, and Kate knew the midnight passenger train was due. In the pitch dark, she made her way along muddy tracks, crawled over a trestle across the river, and ran a mile to raise the alarm. She was gifted a scholarship to college and, rather fittingly, had a bridge named after her.

7ᵗʰ July 1941

Maureen 'Paddy' O'Sullivan joined Britain's Women's Auxiliary Air Force and then the Special Overseas Executive, an underground spy unit. The Dubliner parachuted into the south of France in March 1944 (her fall cushioned by the two million francs in her backpack). She set herself up as a wireless operator, cycling 60km a day between hidden radio sets. Blessed with the gift of the gab, on more than one occasion she was able to charm German soldiers into accepting dates instead of searching her bags.

8ᵗʰ July 1979

The Sunday Game launched on RTÉ One with its first woman GAA pundit, Liz Howard. In the 1970s, a woman pundit for the national sport was really blazing a trail. Liz had won an impressive five All-Ireland camogie medals; she was PRO for Tipperary GAA for more than twenty years and then president of the Camogie Association. It seems only right that, during her term as president, RTÉ added camogie coverage to *The Sunday Game*.

9th July 1959

The first dozen bean gardaí – female recruits – joined the Garda Síochána, with Galway's Mary Browne top of the list as Garda 00001W. On their first day on the beat, a woman garda was such an odd sight that people literally stopped in the street to look at them. Some locals fondly called them 'the bandy guards'.

10th July 1949

Dr Dorothy Stopford Price was appointed head of the National BCG Committee. The Dubliner specialised in the treatment of tuberculosis, one of the major causes of death in Ireland at the time. Dorothy trialled the BCG vaccine in 1938 before it was rolled out across the country. It led to the complete eradication of TB here, saving countless lives – and making Dorothy an unsung hero.

11th July 1854

Mount Lola in California was named for the actor and dancer Lola Montez, who had entertained thousands there during the gold rush. Born in Sligo as Elizabeth Gilbert, she debuted in London at twenty-two years of age with her new stage name. She would become known around the world for her risqué Spider Dance (with a finale showing she wasn't wearing bloomers). She was fiercely intelligent and refused to accept the morals of the 1800s. Many now think of her as one of the first women liberationists.

12th July 2023

Emma Dabiri was elected a fellow of the Royal Society of Literature. The bestselling author explores race and cultural appropriation in her books, including *Don't Touch My Hair* and *What White People Can Do Next*. Emma's sense of social justice was evident even as a young child growing up in Dublin. At the age of seven, when her classmates were studying for their First Communion, she wrote a 'spiffy little anti-slavery pamphlet' which she presented to her teachers.

13th July 2014

Two acclaimed women directors shared the award for Best Documentary at the Galway Film Fleadh. Sinead O'Brien's *Blood Fruit* told the story of the Dunnes workers who refused to handle South African goods in the 1980s. Aoife Kelleher's *One Million Dubliners* explored the history of Glasnevin Cemetery and the lives of the characters, living and dead, connected with it. It went on to be named *The Irish Times*'s Best Irish Film of 2014.

14th July 1999

Fidelma Macken was the first woman nominated as a judge for the European Court of Justice; she was appointed later that year. Born and raised in Dublin, she became a barrister and then a High Court judge. On her return to Ireland, she was promoted to the Supreme Court. Her upbringing was key to her success: 'I grew up not realising that there was any distinction to be drawn between boys and girls or men and women in terms of what you might want to do with your life.'

15th July 2015

The Gender Recognition Act was finally passed by the Irish government after a mammoth twenty-two-year legal battle by transgender woman Dr Lydia Foy. Born in Westmeath, Lydia has lived as a woman since 1991.

She first applied for a birth certificate that accurately reflected her gender back in 1993. Once the Act was passed, Lydia was the first person to receive a Gender Recognition Certificate issued in Ireland.

16th July 1903

Elizabeth 'Lolly' Yeats published her first book under the Cuala Press imprint. Lolly was an outspoken feminist; her sister Lily was more reserved but no less talented. Together they set up Cuala Industries, a landmark collective for crafts and publishing. Lily specialised in embroidery, Lolly in books. They employed only women and used only Irish materials, and were an important part of the Celtic Revival.

17th July 1908

Beatrice Hill-Lowe began two days of archery events at the Olympics in London. She would become the first Irish woman to win an Olympic medal. Archery was the only competitive sport open to women back then, since it didn't involve the exertion of running and they could remain fully clothed. A t-shirt and a pair of shorts and all hell would break loose.

18th July 1974

The Ladies' Gaelic Football Association was officially founded at Hayes Hotel in Thurles, County Tipperary. That first year, just eight counties took part in the All-Ireland senior championship – four of them from Munster. Each county paid £10 to cover the cost of the medals. The final was a hard-fought contest, with Tipperary beating Offaly by just a point.

19th July 1984

Dunnes Stores employees Mary Manning and Karen Gearon refused to handle South African grapefruits. The women were following a union directive, in protest at the Apartheid regime. They were suspended and, together with nine co-workers, went out on strike. Their protest went on for nearly three years, during which they lived on just £21 a week in strike pay. On his visit to Dublin in 1990, Nelson Mandela met the strikers to show his gratitude.

20th July 1974

A group calling themselves the Dublin City Women's Invasion Force arrived at the Forty Foot in Sandycove, County Dublin, to protest the men-only swimming at this popular bathing spot. The group included journalist Nell McCafferty, politician Nuala Fennell, and poet Mary D'Arcy, who arrived by currach (how else?). Since their protest, women have routinely swum at the Forty Foot. But it's only within the last decade they could become full members of the Sandycove Bathers' Association.

21st July 2022

The Mayor of Washington, DC, declared this day to be

'Mary O'Toole Day', honouring the US's first woman municipal judge. Mary was born in Hacketstown, County Carlow, and emigrated with her aunt and uncle at the age of sixteen. She became a stenographer before going on to study the law. As the first woman appointed to the bench in 1921, her seal of office had to be amended by hand, crossing out the 'his' and writing in 'hers'.

22nd July 2008

Greatest-hits album *The Galway Girl: The Best of Sharon Shannon* was released. One of Ireland's foremost accordion players, Sharon was born in County Clare. She was performing by the age of eight and touring the US at fourteen. Her debut album is the best-selling traditional music album ever released in Ireland. After more than thirty years in the business, she insists, 'I'll never stop being blown away by Irish music.'

23rd July 1903

Mary 'Mother' Jones led the March of the Mill Children into New York. The Cork-born trade unionist and hundreds of mine workers were demanding a 55-hour working week and better conditions for child workers. Mary had emigrated to Canada, then the US, where she spent her life fighting for workers' rights. She was labelled 'the most dangerous woman in America' by a district attorney and fondly nicknamed 'Mother' by the union members. Eye of the beholder.

24th July 1924

The Seanad debated the awarding of pensions to women who fought in the War of Independence or Civil War. In the end, Dr Brigid Lyons was the only woman to be granted a pension under the 1924 law. Brigid had taken a break from studying medicine to join the Rising. She was the first woman commissioned in the Irish Defence Forces, as Commandant – and the only woman commissioned until 1981.

25th July 2011

Susan Denham was appointed Ireland's first woman Chief Justice. The Dublin lawyer studied at Trinity and King's Inns and was involved with the Free Legal Advice Centres. She was called to the Bar in 1971 and often found herself the only woman in a courtroom. She was the first woman to serve on the Supreme Court in 1992. That year, she was the only dissenting voice in a verdict against abortion information.

26th July 1914

Mary Spring Rice arrived in Howth harbour on the *Asgard* with a cargo of guns. The Anglo-Irish aristocrat was an active supporter of the Irish Republican Army. She allowed her family's Limerick estate to be used as a safe house and the family boat for ferrying men and arms over the Shannon Estuary. She used her society connections to pressure politicians to support Irish independence.

27th July 1669

It is thought that the real-life Molly Malone was christened in Dublin on this date. The evidence is unreliable at best, but Molly has become a lasting symbol of the capital. Her statue was unveiled during Dublin's millennium and now stands on Suffolk Street. Of all the statues dotted around Dublin, Molly is one of only half a dozen women depicted.

28th July 1962

Mainie Jellett was celebrated posthumously with an exhibition of her work at the Hugh Lane Gallery. Her first painting teacher was none other than Lolly Yeats. As an emerging artist in the 1920s, Mainie was criticised for her dangerous foreign notions – she often combined abstract art with old religion and Celtic design. Now, she is considered one of Ireland's first modernists.

29th July 1848

Lady Jane Wilde, under her pen name Speranza, published a call for armed revolt in *The Nation*. The journal was closed down and the editor tried for sedition. When Jane stood up in court and claimed responsibility, she was ignored. A significant literary and political figure, she collected Irish folktales for posterity. She was a chronicler of the Famine and a fierce campaigner for better education for women.

30th July 1933

The final of the first All-Ireland Camogie Championship got underway. Ten counties took part that year, though Wexford had struggled to field a team. The women wore knee-length gym frocks, long black socks and canvas boots. Dublin beat Galway by nine points in the final to secure the O'Duffy Cup. The first thirteen camogie championship titles were won by either Dublin or Cork.

31st July 1973

At long last, legislation ended the marriage bar in the Irish civil service. For nearly fifty years, women had been forced to leave the service when they married. This had been justified by everything from the unfairness of two-income households to the impropriety of pregnant women teaching. It was illegal under European law, and Ireland was one of the last countries to lift the ban.

AUGUST

1st **August** 1949

TV news footage showed Iris Kellett winning the Princess Elizabeth Cup at the International Horse Show in London. It was Europe's most prestigious women's event at the time, and she would win it again two years later. Though small in stature, Iris was a fearless showjumper. She became one of the most influential figures in Irish equestrian sport, training many of our most famous showjumpers. She held herself with dignity and was highly respected, and almost always addressed as 'Miss Kellett'.

2nd **August** 1988

The first ever all-woman Aer Lingus crew left Dublin. The pilot was Captain Gráinne Cronin and the co-pilot Elaine Egan. Gráinne had trained in England before becoming Aer Lingus's first female pilot in 1978. Ireland's airline was only the second in the world to recruit women. These days, about 11% of Aer Lingus pilots are women.

3rd **August** 2018

Katie-George Dunlevy and Eve McCrystal became double para-cycling Road World Champions for the second year in a row. Katie-George is visually impaired, with a progressive eye condition. Born in the UK to an Irish father, she competes for Ireland. She and pilot Eve have a huge haul of medals for tandem events, including gold at the Rio and Tokyo Paralympics. Her advice to her younger self would be: 'Great things can happen. Just believe in yourself and there are things you can do.'

4th **August** 2022

The IRFU announced professional contracts for women's 15s players for the first time. These were in addition to the contracts already in place with the women's Sevens players. It was a welcome move for elite women's rugby – though the financial terms were significantly less than for their male counterparts.

5th **August** 2018

The Irish women's hockey team walked out onto the pitch for the final of the World Cup in London. They had defied all expectations to get there. The lowest-ranked team in the tournament, they had gone on a dream run to beat the US, India and Spain. Vital to their success was Antrim goalkeeper Ayeisha McFerran, who pulled off save after save. She won herself Goalkeeper of the Tournament.

6th **August** 2014

Christina Noble won the prestigious Albert Schweitzer Leadership for Life Award. Christina grew up in poverty in Dublin's Liberties and an orphanage in the west of Ireland. After a visit to Vietnam, she founded the Christina Noble Children's Foundation to help those in the country affected by poverty. She later expanded her work to help families in Mongolia. Her foundation has helped over 700,000 children.

7th **August** 1982

Maura O'Halloran graduated as a Buddhist Zen master in Japan. She had always been interested in meditation and Buddhism, and at twenty-four she travelled to Tokyo. She proved herself incredibly adept and achieved enlightenment less than six months after becoming a master. She died tragically young, at just twenty-seven. She was given the name 'Great Enlightened Lady, of the same heart and mind as the Great Teacher Buddha'.

8th **August** 1965

A cross was erected at Krosshólaborg, Iceland, to commemorate Aud the Deep-Minded. Aud was a 9th century Norwegian who married to become the Viking Queen of Dublin. She had huge power for a woman of her time. After her husband's death, she fled to Iceland with her grandchildren. She took twenty prisoners to crew the ship and granted them their freedom on arrival. Aud is considered a foremother of the Icelandic nation.

9th August 2012

Boxing legend Katie Taylor won gold at the Olympics in London. Katie was raised in Bray, County Wicklow, and started boxing at the age of eleven. A real trailblazer, she won five consecutive gold medals at the World Championships. She turned professional in 2016 and secured the WBA, IBF and WBO titles. Her Olympic gold was a momentous occasion for Irish sport. Goosebumps.

10th August 1953

Designer Sybil Connolly's ensemble of red cape and white dress appeared on the cover of *Life* magazine alongside the headline 'Irish Invade Fashion World'. Sybil had launched her own Dublin fashion label and her clients included icons Liz Taylor and Jackie

Kennedy. She employed a hundred women, who worked on designs using Irish linen, lace and knitwear. When asked about marriage, she said, 'For the moment, I like to buy my mink and diamonds myself.'

11th August 1942

Cork woman Mary Elmes smuggled nine Jewish children out of a French refugee camp in the boot of her car. They had been destined for a convoy to Auschwitz. The Trinity scholar had volunteered to work with refugees from the Spanish Civil War. Between August and October 1942, she and her colleagues saved 427 children from the Nazis. An unassuming hero, she preferred not to talk about her stunning bravery.

12th August 1995

Sonia O'Sullivan won gold in the 5000m at the World Athletics Championships in Gothenburg. Growing up in Cork, she joined her local athletics club for the discos and the weekends away. But talent can't be kept down, and she soon started notching up the wins. Sonia broke world records and competed in four Olympic games, winning silver in Sydney 2000. She is one of our most successful sportspeople ever.

13th **August** 2023

Dubliner Hannah Tyrrell was player of the match in her county's victory over Kerry in the All-Ireland ladies' football final. The versatile sportswoman has excelled in Gaelic, rugby and soccer. She played on the team that won the Six Nations in 2015 and in two FAI Women's Cup finals. She is also a mental health advocate – and a big fan of resilience. 'Life is about picking yourself back up, dusting yourself off and going again.'

14th **August** 2020

Donegal native Tahlia Britton became the Irish Navy's first female diver, after completing a gruelling eleven-week course with a 70% dropout rate. The twenty-nine-year-old gunnery officer went on to join the elite diving service. She has the requisite nerves of steel for underwater engineering, search-and-rescue missions and even explosive disposals.

15th August 1998

A plaque was erected to Maude Delap on Valentia Island, County Kerry. Born in 1866, Maude had a lifelong interest in sea creatures, especially jellyfish. A citizen scientist, she had a special jellyfish lab which she called 'the department'. She was the first person in history to rear jellyfish in captivity and to study their complicated life cycle in full. The anemone species *Edwardsia delapiae* is named in her honour.

16th August 1878

The Intermediate Education Act allowed women to take exams, earn degrees and enter into professions. It was a revolutionary new law – and women had only been added to the bill in the final stages. Within twenty years, 60% of teachers in Ireland were women (earning 80% of the male wage, because *of course* they were).

17th **August** 1897

Entrepreneur Belinda Mulrooney opened the Grand Forks Hotel in Bonanza Creek during the US gold rush. Belinda had moved to Pennsylvania from Sligo as a teenager. A daring entrepreneur who swore like a trooper, she made money renting out building space. She also bought and sold everything from whiskey to hot water bottles. Then she moved out west and turned to mining. At her height, she was worth over $1 million.

18th **August** 1882

The Married Women's Property Act finally allowed women to own property. The new law owed a lot to campaigning by Scottish-Ulster suffragist Isabella Tod. Isabella founded Northern Ireland's suffrage society and lobbied Queen's University until it admitted female students. She also campaigned for the dignified treatment of sex workers. She believed 'the world is unspeakably harder to a woman who falls than a man, and doors of escape which stand open to him are closed to her'.

19th August 1861

Anne Jellicoe co-founded the Dublin branch of the Society for Promoting the Employment of Women. Anne was born in County Laois and fought all her life for equal access to education. She founded Alexandra College, Dublin, to offer advanced education for women. The college helped persuade Trinity College to allow women to sit exams there, paving the way for the full admission of women.

20th August 1928

Sara Allgood gave a sensational performance in *Juno and the Paycock* at the Abbey Theatre. The Dubliner was one of the greatest character actors of her time. She studied acting with the Daughters of Ireland and began her career at the Abbey. She appeared in numerous films, scoring an Oscar nomination for best supporting actress in *How Green Was My Valley*. A fellow actor once said Sara's voice 'was gold and silver, and if so she wished, iron'.

21st August 1797

Irishwoman Deh-he-wä-mis took part in negotiations for the Treaty of Big Tree. She was born Mary Jemison aboard a ship from Belfast to Pennsylvania. At fifteen, she was captured by a Shawnee raiding party. Rather than being ransomed back to the British, she chose to live among the Iroquois nations. When the British abandoned their alliance, the tribe were forced to sell much of their land through an infamous series of treaties. An astute negotiator, Deh-he-wä-mis was allotted 18,000 acres of land near New York.

22nd August 1861

Social worker Ellen Woodlock presented an expert paper on the relief of impoverished children. Ellen had spent her life working for Ireland's disadvantaged. She partnered with Sarah Atkinson to set up a children's hospital on Dublin's Buckingham Street. It had just eight beds when it opened but grew rapidly. It moved to its current premises at Temple Street in 1872.

23rd August 1881

Philanthropist Lucinda Sullivan died in the nursing home that she had founded. The Limerick woman had dedicated her life to caring for others. She had been the first lady superintendent of the Adelaide Hospital in Dublin. An expert fundraiser, she then set up a home for children with spinal and joint diseases. The first institution of its kind in Ireland, its name was later changed to Sunbeam House.

24th August 2012

Kildare comedian Aisling Bea won So You Think You're Funny? at the Edinburgh Fringe. Since then, her career has gone from strength to strength – as a stand-up comedian, an actor and a panellist on shows like *QI*. She writes and stars in the brilliant, BAFTA-winning drama *This Way Up*. A firm believer in gender equality, she says, 'Women can do pretty much everything a man can do except for slapping the roof of a car to say "On you go" when somebody is driving away.'

25th August 1932

Nancy Corrigan broke a world solo flying record in Cleveland, Ohio. The Achill native had had less than five hours of flight lessons but insisted, 'I wasn't a bit afraid. It felt like a million dollars.' She worked as a fashion model in New York to finance her burgeoning pilot career. She went on to train US fighter pilots during World War II. Later, as head of a flying school in Missouri, she guided six hundred women through their programme.

26th August 2021

Dubliner Ellen Keane won gold in the 100m breaststroke at the Tokyo Paralympics. Born with an underdeveloped left arm, she became Ireland's youngest Paralympian at just thirteen. She is amassing quite the collection of World Championship and Paralympics medals. In 2017, she gave a TEDx Talk on looking at her disability differently, called 'My Lucky Fin'.

27th August 1923

Kathleen Lynn refused to take her Dáil seat in protest against the Treaty. The Mayo woman was Chief

Medical Officer of the Irish Citizen Army during the Rising. Not just a medic, she used her own car to run guns into Dublin. A few years later, she and partner Madeleine ffrench-Mullen founded St. Ultan's Children's Hospital. When she died, she had both a nurses' guard of honour and a full military funeral.

28th August 1812

Anna Doyle Wheeler left her abusive husband and went on to establish herself as an early feminist thinker. She gave public talks in London and collaborated with Irishman William Thompson on a groundbreaking book on women's rights. She argued that treating women as little more than 'beasts of burden' meant that men would miss out on the company of independent, educated women. As relevant now as in the 1800s.

29th August 2007

Atonement opened the Venice Film Festival, with

a breakthrough performance from twelve-year-old Saoirse Ronan. It earned her a supporting actress Oscar nomination, making her one of the youngest nominees ever. Born in the Bronx, she has lived in Ireland since the age of three. By twenty-six, she had scored three more Oscar nominations, for best actress in *Brooklyn*, *Lady Bird* and *Little Women*. Despite growing up on film sets, she never really felt like a child actor, 'just an actor who happened to be quite young'.

30th August 2018

Sally Rooney's second novel, *Normal People*, was published to wide acclaim. It tells the story of the complex relationship between Sligo teenagers Marianne and Connell. It won the Costa Book Award and has been published in nearly fifty languages. It was the follow-up to her hugely successful debut, *Conversations with Friends*. With minimalist, assured writing, Sally has been heralded as one of the great millennial novelists.

31st August 1910

Lilian Bland was the first woman in the world to design, build and pilot a plane. Unconventional for her time, Lilian wore breeches, tinkered around with cars and was one of the first women sports journalists. At Randalstown, County Antrim, she made her first successful flight, staying thirty feet off the ground for a quarter of a mile. Her fuel tank was made from a whiskey bottle, and the fuel funnel from her aunt's ear trumpet. She named her plane *Mayfly* because 'it may fly or it may not'.

SEPTEMBER

1st **September** 2019

A new edition of Mary Ward's classic book *Sketches with the Microscope* was released. It was first published in 1857. A gifted artist, Mary was given a microscope at eighteen years of age, and it changed her life. She collected plants and insects and made her own slides from slivers of ivory, drawing the intricate images she saw. She amassed a huge knowledge of botany, entomology and microscopy – at a time before women were allowed to undertake formal study.

2nd **September** 2013

Dublin City Council voted to name the newest Liffey bridge after Rosie Hackett, making it the first of Dublin's many bridges to be named for a woman. Rosie grew up in the inner city, in a house her family shared with four others. At eighteen, she started work at Jacob's biscuit factory and became heavily involved in trade unionism. She co-founded the Irish Women

Workers' Union in 1911. She was a strident republican and occupied Stephen's Green with Countess Markievicz during the Rising. Despite her lifetime as a truly great trade union leader, the occupation on Rosie's death certificate reads 'spinster'.

3rd September 2021

The movie *The Lost Daughter* premiered, with Killarney actor Jessie Buckley playing a younger version of Olivia Colman's character. The role would garner Jessie an Oscar nomination for supporting actress. Since first coming to the public eye in the BBC talent show *I'd Do Anything*, she has built an impressive career with roles in musicals, theatre and film. She loves the idea of reclaiming women's stories: 'We're not a second-class citizen who took a bite out of an apple and was cursed for the rest of time.'

4th **September** 2017

Zainab Boladale was introduced as Ireland's first Afro-Irish TV presenter. She moved with her family from Lagos, Nigeria, to Ennis, County Clare, at the age of three. Zainab has always loved hearing people's stories and gravitated towards journalism. She joined the crew of RTÉ children's show *news2day* and then moved to *Nationwide*. She particularly loves 'learning about other people's definition of "woman" and how they've shaped their "womanliness" to fit them'.

5th **September** 1917

Louise Gavan Duffy fulfilled a personal ambition with the opening of an Irish-speaking girls' school, Scoil Bhríde in St. Stephen's Green. Louise was active in the Gaelic revival, the suffrage movement and the nationalist cause. When she heard that the Rising was happening, she strode into the GPO to express her opposition to Patrick Pearse and warn of the certain loss of life. Nonetheless, she took up her place helping in the kitchen on the top floor and was one of the last to leave with the wounded. In the aftermath, she was painstaking in delivering messages to the families of the imprisoned men.

6th **September** 1593

Grace 'Granuaile' O'Malley met Elizabeth I in Greenwich Palace in London. She negotiated the release of her son, who was being held captive by the Governor of Connacht. A chieftain's daughter, Granuaile grew up to be a fearless sea captain and pirate queen. Legend has it that she gave birth to one of her sons in the middle of a sea battle. She was back leading her crew, baby in her arms, within the hour.

7th **September** 1933

Thirty women met in Dublin to form the Irish Women Writers' Club. Dorothy Macardle was its first president and mentor for younger writers. The Dundalk teacher was affectionately known by her students as 'Maccy' before she was dismissed for her republican activities. She worked as both playwright and journalist, and wrote gothic novels. Her best-known work was the chilling ghost story *Uneasy Freehold*, later known as *The Uninvited*. Not for the faint-hearted.

8th September 2022

Anne O'Leary stepped down as CEO of Vodafone Ireland and went on to become Meta Ireland's new CEO. Her management style is progressive and inclusive. At Vodafone, she boosted female representation across the company. It was one of the first companies in Ireland to introduce a policy of support for domestic violence survivors and additional leave for both fertility treatment and pregnancy loss.

9th September 2021

Award-winning company Izzy Wheels announced a collaboration with Disney. Two sisters, Ailbhe and Izzy Keane, founded the company in 2016. Izzy has spina bifida and has been a wheelchair user all her life. The sisters create specially designed wheel covers that match the user's personality. They've worked with designers and brands from all over the world, including Barbie. Their motto is, 'If you can't stand up, stand out!'

10th September 2023

Tyrone astronomer Annie Maunder had an asteroid named after her. Annie studied at Cambridge but, as a woman in 1889, wasn't allowed to graduate. She became a 'lady computer' at the Greenwich Observatory and discovered a link between sunspots and the Earth's climate. She was forced to retire when she married but still published work under her husband's name (which he fully acknowledged). As well as her own asteroid,

Annie joins astronomer Agnes Clerke in having a moon crater named for her.

11th September 1956

Saint Joan opened on Broadway with legendary actor Siobhán McKenna in the lead – her most iconic role. Born in Belfast, Siobhán spoke Irish growing up. She was taken on by the Abbey Theatre, often for Irish-language parts at first. She played a wide range of roles on the stage, in film and on TV, and was the first Irish actor to win a Tony award. At her funeral, Brian Friel declared, 'For people of my generation, she personified an idea of Ireland.'

12th September 2004

Costume designer Consolata Boyle won an Emmy for her work on *The Lion in Winter*. Consolata studied history but was lured over to costume design and textiles instead. She worked on classic films like *Into the West*, *The Snapper* and *The Queen*. She says 'I've been lucky to be involved in stories and films about women. Whether I like the women or despise them or question them or love them, all of them have been completely fascinating to investigate.'

13th September 1979

Jennifer Johnston's *The Old Jest* was published. It went on to win the Whitbread Prize and was adapted into an award-winning film. The story is of a young Protestant girl who finds an IRA commander hiding in a nearby beach house. Jennifer grew up in Dublin but lived for decades in Derry. Impressively prolific, she is one of the leading Irish novelists of her generation. She won the lifetime achievement at the Irish Book Awards in 2012.

14th September 2022

The Free Contraception Scheme was introduced for

women aged 17–25. It was later expanded to include women, transgender and non-binary people up to the age of 35. It was finally an official acknowledgement of the cost of contraception – and that it's most often paid for by women.

15th September 2019

The All-Ireland ladies' football final had a record-breaking crowd of 56,114. It was the largest attendance ever at a women's amateur sports event in Europe. TV viewing figures are on the rise too, with about 600,000 people tuning into the live 2021 final. In the last twenty years, the number of ladies' Gaelic clubs and members has more than doubled.

16th September 2021

The National Ploughing Championships celebrated its ninetieth anniversary. For more than half that time, Anna May McHugh has been at the helm.

The Laois woman joined the association as secretary, then managing director. Under her leadership, 'The Ploughing' has become Europe's largest event of its kind. Anna May described herself as just a small cog in the machine but does admit that she 'made the wheel go faster'.

17th **September** 2013

Anne Anderson became Ireland's first woman ambassador to the US. From Clonmel, Anne joined the foreign service straight out of university. She worked her way up the rungs and then started breaking glass ceilings. As well as the US, she was our first woman ambassador to the EU and to France. Anne has spoken about the generations of skilled women diplomats who never had the chance to do the same, due to the now infamous marriage bar.

18th September 1877

Elizabeth Blackburne's book, *Illustrious Irishwomen*, was published in London. It was the first collection of Irish women's biographies of its type. It covered a cast of formidable characters, from Henrietta Boyle to St. Brigid, Maria Edgeworth to Queen Macha. Elizabeth was a novelist from Slane, County Meath. She said that compiling the book was 'the silent patriotism of my life'.

19th September 2022

Síofra O'Leary was elected the first female president of the European Court of Human Rights. A UCD graduate, Síofra spent twenty years at the EU's Court of Justice. Her time at the ECHR has seen her deal with cases on everything from climate action to Russia's invasion of Ukraine.

20th September 1949

Ireland was represented at the UNESCO general

assembly in Paris by Josephine McNeill. From Fermoy, County Cork, Josephine was active in both Cumann na mBan and the Irish Countrywomen's Association. For her diplomatic career, she is said to have suppressed her rebel tendencies and channelled her inner public servant. She became Ireland's first woman head of mission when she was appointed minister to the Netherlands in the 1950s. She paved the way for the twenty-four women ambassadors in Irish embassies around the world today.

21st September 2022

The Ellen Hutchins Building at University College Cork was officially named for this early botanist. Ellen died in 1815 at just twenty-nine years old, but in her short life, she identified and catalogued hundreds of plants near her Bantry home. With a keen eye and deep knowledge, her legacy remains in the three types of lichen, two algae and two mosses named after her.

22nd September 1914

Pioneering radiologist Florence Stoney led an all-women surgical unit to Antwerp to establish a war hospital. Her offer to provide medical services to the War Office had been rebuffed, but she got a team together and went anyway. The Dubliner was later appointed Head of Radiology at Fulham Military Hospital and specialised in locating bullets and shrapnel.

23rd September 2008

Singer-songwriter Imelda May's big break came with her first appearance on *Later with Jools Holland*. Hailing from Dublin's Liberties, Imelda started performing at the age of sixteen. Since then, she has become one of Ireland's most acclaimed artists, selling millions of records. 'There have never been so many women in the music industry, but they're doing ballads and pop … I wanna be the woman that rocks.' And she does.

24th September 1928

Ninette de Valois's Abbey Theatre School of Ballet began a run of performances after its founding that year. The Wicklow woman toured with the famous Ballets Russes and went on to found the Royal Ballet in London. After setting up the Abbey School of Ballet, she worked on productions with a range of Irish composers and artists. She is widely recognised as the architect of Irish ballet.

25th September 2016

Cork's ladies' Gaelic footballers won their sixth All-Ireland final in a row. The team included dual players Briege Corkery and Rena Buckley. Over their careers, the massively talented pair won thirty-six All-Ireland senior medals between them. That's an unprecedented haul of eleven football medals and seven camogie medals each. Evenly matched for skills and achievement, the two were jointly awarded Sportswoman of the Year in 2015.

26th September 1995

Dundalk band The Corrs released their first album, *Forgiven, Not Forgotten* – and the world fell head over heels for their blend of traditional Irish themes and catchy pop. The three sisters – Andrea, Sharon and Caroline – and brother Jim started out playing in their aunt's pub and ended up selling forty million albums worldwide. At one point, they held the top two positions in the UK album charts. Sibling revelry.

27th September 1992

A Woman's Heart started its eighth week in a row at No. 1 in the Irish album charts. It was knocked off the top spot for a few weeks before planting itself back there for another run. It comprised a dozen tracks by artists Eleanor McEvoy (who wrote the title track), sisters Mary Black and Frances Black, Dolores Keane, Sharon Shannon and Maura O'Connell. It is often cited as the best-selling Irish album of all time.

28th September 1997

Catherina McKiernan won the Berlin marathon. It was the fastest ever debut marathon by a woman. She was the first Irish woman to win the London marathon the following year. The Cavan athlete set eight national records over her career, some of which are still to be broken. Since retiring, she now runs just for the love of it. 'Sure, isn't it an addiction? Once a runner, always a runner.'

29th September 2021

Dr Maeve O'Rourke spoke about addressing historical abuses at the Women as Legal Changemakers conference in Belfast. Maeve is based at the Irish Centre for Human Rights in University of Galway. She works pro bono for survivors of Ireland's institutions. She is the legal expert for the Justice for Magdalenes campaign, and helped secure the State apology and redress scheme.

30th September 1997

The close of nominations for the Irish presidency saw four women out of five nominees. This owed much to the outstanding popularity of Ireland's first woman president, Mary Robinson. The candidates included anti-nuclear campaigner Adi Roche and singer Dana Rosemary Scallon. Mary McAleese would go on to win with more than 45% of the first vote.

OCTOBER

1st **October** 1846

Artist and collector Lady Harriet Kavanagh departed on an eighteen-month tour of the Middle East. She was the first Irishwoman to travel around Egypt, much of it on camel-back. She brought three of her children with her, including her youngest son, Arthur, who was born without limbs. Harriet always fostered Arthur's independence, commissioning a mechanical wheelchair and teaching him to write and paint by mouth.

2nd **October** 1982

The Republic of Ireland women's football team scored their first competitive win, against Northern Ireland. The Women's FAI was set up in 1973, and slowly but surely, momentum has been building. The team narrowly missed out on qualification for the Euros in 2022 and finally made it to their first World Cup in 2023. Onwards and upwards. COYGIG!

3rd **October** 1854

Soprano Catherine Hayes gave an acclaimed
performance in Sydney, Australia. Born into poverty
in Limerick, she trained in Dublin and Paris. She was
the first Irish woman to sing at the Royal Opera in
London and Milan's La Scala. She performed all over
the world and became a full-on global superstar. Fans
loved her sweet voice and amazing vocal range. And by
all accounts, she had an excellent trill.

4th **October** 1980

Mary FitzGerald's arts and crafts segment debuted on
RTÉ One's Saturday morning kids show *Anything Goes*.
Its popularity spawned Mary's own programme, *How
Do You Do?*, which ran for seven years at the turn of the
1990s and helped re-purpose every empty washing-up
bottle and toilet roll in the country. It regularly topped
the ratings and made Mary an instantly recognisable
personality.

5th October 2003

Mayo won the All-Ireland ladies' football final for the fourth time in five years. Their star player was forward Cora Staunton. Cora played her first match at senior level when she was just thirteen and went on to have an outstanding career with her club and county. In 2017, she moved down under to take up Australian Rules Football professionally. She relishes being a role model: 'You don't have to conform to what is considered "the norm" … Be true to yourself.'

6th October 1980

Mella Carroll was appointed the first woman judge in the High Court of Ireland. She went on to become one of its longest-serving judges. Strong-minded and independent, she delivered rulings on a number of controversial cases on abortion information, equal pay and single mothers. For a decade, she was addressed in court as 'My Lord' before expressing a preference for 'Judge'.

7th **October** 1886

Leonora Barry attended the General Assembly of the Knights of Labor. She was the only woman to hold office in the massive US labour union. Leonora had emigrated from Cork with her family when she was just three. She became involved in trade unionism while working at a knitting factory. She battled against sexual harassment and for decent working conditions and equal pay for women. As a direct result of her efforts, Pennsylvania passed its first Factory Inspection Act.

8th **October** 1961

Legendary camogie player Kay Mills led Dublin to victory over Tipperary. It was her fifteenth All-Ireland win, her final game in a Dublin jersey AND her 38th birthday. From Inchicore, Kay made her Dublin debut at sixteen and won her first All-Ireland the following year. When she retired, she was the most decorated player in the history of Gaelic games.

9th October 1979

Cork woman Josie Airey won her case for free legal aid in the European Court of Human Rights. Josie couldn't afford the £1,000 needed to legally separate from her husband. She fought for years to have the law changed, with one Mary Robinson as her legal counsel. Josie's win allowed her separation and granted her £3,140 in damages. It also forced the government to introduce free legal aid before the end of the year.

10th October 2008

Ann Louise Gilligan and Katherine Zappone published their story, *Our Lives Out Loud.* The two had fallen in love in Boston in the early 1980s – when it was still illegal to be gay here in Ireland. They married in Canada in 2003 but lost their constitutional case to have their union recognised here. They founded the action group Marriage Equality, a driving force for a 'Yes' vote in the 2015 Marriage Referendum.

11th **October** 2019

Confidential helpline the Dublin Lesbian Line celebrated its fortieth anniversary. In 1980, Joni Crone had appeared on *The Late Late Show* to publicise the helpline, where she volunteered. She was the first Irish woman to come out as gay on national TV. She wanted to speak up for those 'who had been forced to lead secret lives in shame for too long'. It would be another thirteen years before homosexuality was decriminalised here.

12th **October** 1997

Monaghan Gaelic footballer Brenda McAnespie lined out for her county's second All-Ireland title in a row. She was fourteen weeks pregnant at the time. 'I wanted to play football for Monaghan, and I wanted to have a large family, and there was no reason why it had to be one or the other.' Brenda's Emyvale team later won the 2008 All-Ireland intermediate club final, with her two daughters as teammates. Keeping it in the family.

13th October 1978

Thousands of women marched through Dublin as a Reclaim the Night protest. They carried flaming torches and banners: 'Women Against Violence Against Women'. A speaker announced that the Dublin Rape Crisis Centre would open that month. The march was a powerful expression of Irish women's fear and anger and a demand for change.

14th October 1928

Daisy 'Toto' Bannard Cogley co-founded Dublin's Gate Theatre. The Paris-born actor, director and costume designer would be involved in the running of the theatre for nearly forty years. She had previously run the successful cabaret show The Radical Club and established the Wexford Opera Society. She was active in the suffrage, nationalist and labour movements, and a close associate of Countess Markievicz. Driven, ambitious and idealistic, she was once described as a 'Parisian atom bomb'.

15th October 1988

Enya's 'Orinoco Flow' was released, destined to become her bestselling single. Enya was born into an Irish-speaking Donegal home and only learned English when she started school. As a musician, she became known for her trademark multi-layered sound. Her vocal range is about four octaves. Her commercial range was about 75 million albums.

16th October 1945

The Save the German Children Society was founded in Dublin. Its first chair was paediatrician Kathleen Murphy. In the aftermath of World War II, Kathleen's mission was to find Irish foster homes for five hundred German child refugees. They included orphans and children whose parents were homeless, ill or prisoners of war. The German Gratitude Fund later sent a bronze fountain, which still stands in St. Stephen's Green.

17th October 2020

Pamela Lee and Cat Hunt set a new record for circumnavigating Ireland. They sailed the 761 nautical miles in 92.5 hours, finishing at Kish Lighthouse off the coast of Dublin. With just two of them (instead of a normal crew of up to eight), there were complex navigation and sail changes. The pair worked two hours on and two off for the entire journey. And no doubt slept for Ireland afterwards.

18th October 2012

Cherish (later One Family) celebrated its fortieth anniversary. Founded by Maura O'Dea Richards and five other single mothers, its first president was none other than Mary Robinson. It fought for the fair treatment of separated and single mothers back when women were shunned for having a child out of wedlock. The name 'Cherish' came from the 1916 Proclamation that Ireland would 'cherish all of the children of the nation equally'.

19th October 1999

The biggest strike in Ireland's history began, with 27,500 nurses (mostly women) demanding better pay and working conditions. At the time, the most a nurse could earn was £30,000, no matter their experience or level of training. After eight days of strike action, the government offered a number of key concessions, including the creation of new, more senior posts. Vital progress for a vital workforce.

20th October 2013

Stephanie Roche's goal for Peamount United was captured on camera and became an international sensation. The striker controlled a cross, flicked the ball over her head and whipped it into the net from twenty yards out. Stephanie's skill earned her runner-up in FIFA's goal of the year. She took all the accompanying media madness in her stride. The Shamrock Rovers player now has an impressive fifty international caps.

21st October 1964

Máiréad Ní Ghráda's best known play, *An Trial*, was shown on TV. The Clare playwright studied Irish in UCD and wrote radio and stage scripts as well as books. She also worked for the underground Irish government and in 1921 was jailed for selling republican flags on Grafton Street. She later became Raidió Éireann's principal announcer – the first woman in Europe to hold such a job on a national broadcaster.

22nd October 1884

The first nine women graduated from the Royal University of Ireland. They were the first women to graduate anywhere in Ireland and Britain and became known as the 'Nine Graces'. They included Isabella Mulvany, the headmistress of Alexandra College, where many of the graduates had studied. Their degrees ranged from literature and music to philosophy and metaphysics.

23rd October 2020

Front Line Defenders hosted a unique interview with Ireland's three United Nations Special Rapporteurs at the time. These are independent experts who report to the UN on human rights. Mary Lawlor specialises in human rights defenders, Siobhán Mullally in human trafficking, and Fionnuala Ní Aoláin in protecting rights while countering terrorism. The three have spent their careers protecting human rights globally. Extraordinary women, all.

24th October 1910

Mary Ryan began her first academic year as Professor of Romance Languages at University College Cork. She was the first woman professor in Ireland or Britain, and her promotion of French culture won her the country's Legion of Honour. Mary was always mindful of her role as a mentor to female students. When she retired in 1939, women made up nearly 30% of the student body.

25th October 1996

The last Magdalene Laundry, on Dublin's Sean MacDermott Street, closed its doors for good. Seventeen years later, Taoiseach Enda Kenny would issue a state apology for the horrifying treatment of the ten thousand girls and women forced to live in the laundries. Run by the Catholic Church, they were supported by the Irish state from its foundation. Kenny called it 'a national shame'. The apology was long overdue but deeply felt.

26th October 1906

Galwegian Alice Perry was the first woman in Europe awarded a civil engineering degree. She was the first Irish woman to become a county surveyor when she temporarily succeeded her father. But when the job came up as a permanent position, she lacked the requisite age and experience. She was forced to emigrate to London, where she worked as a factory inspector. In 2017, NUI Galway officially named their Alice Perry Engineering Building.

27th October 1989

Louise Kennedy was named Irish Designer of the Year. She launched her first collection at just twenty-three with a bank loan of €10,000. In 1990, she designed the striking purple suit Mary Robinson wore for her presidential inauguration. Since then, she has designed everything from tailored suits to jewellery, Aer Lingus uniforms to law court judges' robes.

28th October 1997

Irishwoman Catherine O'Leary was officially exonerated of any blame for the Great Chicago Fire of 1871. It had taken more than a century for Chicago City Council to set the record straight. At the time, a false rumour spread that Catherine's cow started the fire by kicking over a lantern. Despite findings to the contrary, Catherine, a working-class immigrant, remained vilified. Exoneration of her (and her cow, officially) was well past time.

29th October 1981

The Irish Army's first female platoon passed out (that's 'graduated' to us non-military folk). Thirty-eight young women had signed up for training that included rifle marksmanship and tactics. The 1990s would see the first female officers in the Naval Service and Air Corps.

30th October 1945

The historic Laundry Strike ended after securing a second week's annual holidays for Irish workers. One of the leaders was Louie Bennett of the Irish Women Workers' Union. A lifelong activist, she had always insisted that the IWWU be kept independent of the male unions – to maintain women's priorities. Little known fact: Louie wrote two novels in her thirties. The first was reviewed as 'slightly crude but exceedingly clever and arresting'. #lifegoals

31st **October** 1996

The first volume of Nuala O'Faolain's memoir *Are You Somebody?* was published. It became a *New York Times* bestseller, as did the sequel, *Almost There*, seven years later. Nuala was born in Dublin and worked as a journalist and TV producer for RTÉ and the BBC. Her good friend Marian Finucane called her 'fiercely intelligent, opinionated, articulate to an astonishing degree, erudite, but also loyal, vulnerable and, despite being prone to melancholy, great, great fun'.

NOVEMBER

1st **November** 1921

Averil Deverell was called to the Bar after graduating from Trinity College's Law School. The Wicklow native was the first woman in Ireland and Britain to practise. A barrister for over forty years, she mentored many younger women. She eventually earned the nickname 'Mother of the Bar' as its longest serving member.

2nd **November** 1977

Myrtle Allen's classic *The Ballymaloe Cookbook* was officially launched, and it quickly became a culinary bible in kitchens all over the country. Myrtle championed local, seasonal ingredients at her Michelin-starred Ballymaloe House. She was seen by many as the matriarch of modern Irish cuisine. Her dynasty lives on in daughter-in-law Darina Allen and *her* daughter-in-law Rachel Allen. An impressive female lineage.

3rd **November** 1861

The London Dispatch reported that Catherine Winter's application to vote was denied. She qualified in every way, she was told – except for her gender. Catherine was a formidable woman who didn't shirk from taking on the system. A decade earlier, she had represented herself in a lawsuit to regain possession of a Galway estate. Unintimidated by her surroundings, she coolly questioned witnesses and happily talked back to the judge. A bit fond of long, rambling speeches though ...

4th **November** 1908

The first meeting of the Irish Women's Franchise League took place. The venue was the home of Hanna and Francis Sheehy-Skeffington. When the pair had married, they took each other's names as a sign of equality. Dedicated nationalists, they were both involved in the Rising. When Frank was shot and killed, Hanna refused to accept compensation from the

British Army and demanded an inquiry. She spent the rest of her life campaigning for women's rights and the nationalist cause.

5th **November** 1989

St Paul's of Kilkenny won the All-Ireland Senior Club Camogie Championship for a record eighth time. On the team was one of the greatest camogie players ever, Angela Downey. With her twin sister, Ann, the pair had an intuitive understanding on the field. They would drive the Kilkenny county team to unprecedented dominance in the All-Irelands over twenty years. Angela was named in the Camogie Team of the Century.

6th **November** 2021

The life of Kate Tyrrell was commemorated in a 'Wicklow's Wonder Women' event. Kate was captain of the schooner *Denbighshire Lass* in the 1880s. After inheriting her father's shipping company, Kate fought for a decade to have her name on the ownership documents. Not unlike Granuaile, she was a fearless and charismatic captain. In 1896, she married a childhood friend but kept her maiden name. The scandal.

7th November 1990

Mayo native Mary Robinson was elected Ireland's first woman president. She had a hugely impressive track record in activism and was an incredibly popular president. After her term, she became UN High Commissioner for Human Rights. She is now Chair of the Elders, a group founded by Nelson Mandela to work for peace and justice. In her inauguration speech for president, she thanked 'mná na hÉireann, who instead of rocking the cradle rocked the system'. We've never been prouder.

8th **November** 2012

Maeve Binchy's seventeenth and final novel, *A Week in Winter*, was published posthumously. Her first, *Light a Penny Candle*, was rejected by publishers five times before becoming an instant bestseller. She would go on to huge success as one of Ireland's most beloved writers. Maeve once said that the nicest thing anybody ever called her was a quiet feminist. 'I was absolutely thrilled … I wanted to put that on the cover of every book.'

9th **November** 1911

Katharine Maguire hosted an early meeting of the Association of Registered Medical Women. At the time, there were forty-two women practising medicine in Dublin; Katharine had been the very first and was a huge influence on those who came after her. She opened a free dispensary for women and children and bought and rented out four tenement houses at lowest cost. An obituary read that 'her kindness and sympathy for her patients, especially the poor, were unbounded'.

10th November 1915

Mary 'Pickhandle' Fitzgerald was the first woman elected to Johannesburg City Council. She had emigrated from Wexford to South Africa in her teens. Mary started as a typist for the Mine Workers' Union and was soon involved in union activities. She would eventually become deputy mayor of Johannesburg. She earned her nickname by waving a pickhandle as a weapon in the Black Friday Riots in 1913.

11th November 1997

Mary McAleese was inaugurated for her first term as president. Seven years later, she began her second. Since she succeeded Mary Robinson, Ireland became the first country in the world to have consecutive female presidents. Born in Antrim, Mary McAleese would later be appointed Professor of Law at Trinity College. She used her presidency to, among many other things, build bridges with the Unionist community. A practising Catholic, Mary is fiercely critical of the Church's position on women priests, calling it 'sexist humbug masquerading as threadbare theology'.

12th November 2014

The European Space Agency landed a space probe on a comet for the very first time. The processor that transmitted the data millions of kilometres back to Earth was created here in Ireland. Forty years ago, Professor Susan McKenna-Lawlor founded Space Technology Ireland to build instruments for space travel. The Dublin astrophysicist's creations have been used on missions to the moon, Mars and Mercury.

13th November 1898

Sister Nivedita opened a school for girls in North

Kolkata, India. Born Margaret Noble in County Tyrone, she first made her living by teaching. She became interested in Hinduism and moved to India, where she championed education for girls and women. She is buried in Darjeeling with the epitaph 'Here lies Sister Nivedita who gave her all to India'.

14th November 2015

Marita Conlon-McKenna celebrated the twenty-fifth anniversary of her children's novel *Under the Hawthorn Tree*. Her inspiration for the story came from a radio report about the discovery of an unmarked grave of three Famine-era children. The novel and its two sequels were instant classics and continue to be hugely popular. Dubliner Marita has gone on to write more than twenty much-loved books for children and adults.

15th November 2018

The landmark *Blazing a Trail* exhibition took place

at EPIC museum in Dublin, a collaboration with Herstory. It celebrated the lives of pioneering women, from designer Eileen Gray to sportswoman Mabel Cahill, computer programmer Kay McNulty to trade unionist Mother Jones. Herstory was founded by Melanie Lynch to promote the stories of women that have been overlooked. As she says, 'History without Herstory is half the story.'

16th November 1972

Daphne Pochin Mould's photographic book *Ireland from the Air* was published. The UK-born geologist wrote more than a dozen books, many exploring her strong faith. In her early thirties, she moved to Ireland and learned to fly. She became the country's first woman flight instructor. Daphne loved taking aerial photographs, unnerving passengers by leaning out the window of the plane, hands on camera instead of the controls.

17th November 2016

Playwright Rosaleen McDonagh's *Mainstream* opened at the Project Arts Centre. Rosaleen is a Traveller from Sligo whose groundbreaking book *Unsettled* explored themes of feminism and identity. She was the first ever recipient of the Rowan Award for her lifetime of fighting for human rights and equality. 'Racism, sexism and ableism is my reality. My job is to support all women in the choices they make.'

18th November 2023

The documentary *Croíthe Radacacha* ('Radical Hearts') was screened at The Irish Film Festival in London. Based on research by historian Mary McAuliffe, it told the stories of eight lesbian couples at the centre of the Irish Revolution. They included Margaret Skinnider and Nora O'Keeffe, Kathleen Lynn and Madeleine ffrench-Mullen, and Louie Bennett and Helen Chenevix. Many of the couples would have been dubbed 'lifelong friends who lived together'.

19th November 1940

Two Irish nurses saved the lives of seventeen patients when a London hospital was bombed during World War II. Mary Fleming and Aileen Turner were working in the TB ward of Grove Park Hospital when the bomb hit. They climbed through a first-floor window and crawled across broken glass to rescue the patients before the floor collapsed. They were awarded the George Medal but insisted, 'We were just doing our jobs.'

20th November 1935

Twenty-three-year-old Margaret Haughery arrived in New Orleans by ship. When her husband and young daughter tragically died, Margaret drew on her work ethic and entrepreneurship. She started as a washwoman but soon owned several businesses. She also opened orphanages and a soup kitchen, earning the nickname 'Angel of the Delta'. After her death, New Orleans erected a statue to her, one of the first statues of a woman in the US.

21st **November** 1911

Dr Elizabeth Bell was another suffragist arrested for stone-throwing – in London this time. Elizabeth was Ulster's first woman doctor and one of the first in the British Army's medical corps during World War I. She believed in the universal right to medical treatment, no matter a person's circumstances. She was the doctor for Belfast's Midnight Mission centre for homeless or single mothers and the 'Babies Club' welfare scheme.

22nd **November** 2023

Katriona O'Sullivan's inspiring memoir, *Poor*, scooped not one but two Irish Book Awards. Katriona grew up in Coventry in extreme poverty and surrounded by heroin addiction. She went from teenage pregnancy and homelessness to return to education and graduate with a PhD from Trinity. Now a psychology lecturer, she is a passionate advocate for accessible education for everyone – reaching back to raise others.

23rd **November** 1891

The first class of sixteen students arrived at the Mater Hospital of Nursing. Since then, twenty thousand nurses have graduated and worked on the frontline of medicine. They have battled contagious outbreaks like the Spanish Flu and Covid, and nursed the injured from the 1916 Rising, the Dublin bombings and the Stardust tragedy. To this day, 90% of nurses and midwives in Ireland are women.

24th **November** 1995

Irish voters approved the introduction of divorce into Ireland by the slightest of margins: just 50.28% in favour. Since the 1986 divorce referendum, there had been a substantial increase in separations and a trebling of women claiming the deserted wife's allowance. It had long been one of Ireland's most divisive issues, but divorce finally gave freedom to those in marriages of abuse, desertion or fractured relationships.

25th November 1992

For the first time in its history, the Irish cabinet had two female ministers: Máire Geoghegan-Quinn in Justice and Niamh Bhreathnach in Education. The general election had resulted in a record twenty women TDs. That year, Senator Mary Henry established Group 84, named for her target representation of women in the Houses of the Oireachtas: 84 women out of 220 seats. Even thirty years later, that figure is a considerable way off.

26th November 1862

The first edition of Lady Sydney Morgan's memoirs

was published. Sydney was one of the most talked about literary figures of the 1800s. Best known for *The Wild Irish Girl*, her writing gave her a comfortable independence and access to society's rich and powerful. Her novels were wonderfully controversial, with lashings of Irish patriotism and proto-feminism.

27th November 1962

Film star Maureen O'Sullivan made her Broadway debut at age fifty-one in *Never Too Late*. Born in Boyle, County Roscommon, Maureen was discovered by an American director at the Dublin Horse Show. Her Hollywood career spanned more than seventy films, often earning her particular praise for supporting roles. Her most famous character was Jane in the Tarzan film series, but not everyone was a fan. Her revealing outfits in the first film provoked fury from the Catholic Legion of Decency and were toned down (or covered up) in the sequels.

28th November 1967

Physicist Jocelyn Bell noticed a squiggle on printouts from the massive telescope she had helped build. That squiggle was proof of pulsars, rotating neutron stars. Jocelyn's work would help her (male) supervisor win the Nobel Prize. But the Armagh woman would go on to become a professor and win an array of awards, including the Special Breakthrough Prize in Fundamental Physics. She donated the £2.3 million prize money to scholarships for under-represented groups in physics.

29th November 1956

Kilkenny woman Maeve Kyle took to the track at the Melbourne Olympics for the 100m and 200m. Many admired her as a trailblazer, while others thought her a 'disgraceful hussy' for leaving her husband and child at home. Undaunted, she was Ireland's first woman Olympian and the first Irish person to compete in three Olympics.

30th November 2021

Claire Keegan's *Small Things Like These* was published in the US after a rapturous reception here. A master of short fiction, the Wicklow writer's story *Foster* was adapted as the Oscar-nominated film *An Cailín Ciúin* ('The Quiet Girl'). Bestselling and universally acclaimed, *Small Things Like These* was the shortest book ever nominated for the Booker Prize. As Claire said herself, 'Elegance is saying just enough.'

DECEMBER

1st **December** 1942

Irishwoman Mary 'Claudine' Herbert joined an undercover network in German-occupied France. She spoke five languages, which was useful for assumed identities. Her job was to arrange parachute drops of supplies and safe passage of agents and escapers. She fell in love with the leader of her spy network and the two had a daughter together. In February 1944, she was arrested by the Gestapo and withstood sustained interrogation. She was later reunited with her husband and daughter.

2nd **December** 2010

Nan Joyce received a lifetime achievement award for her work on Travellers' rights. She came to prominence when Gay Byrne broadcast his radio show from the Tallaght halting site where she lived. She went on to write a Travellers' manifesto of rights and needs, and in 1982, she was the first Traveller candidate in a general election.

3rd December 2023

Fionnuala McCormack qualified for the marathon at the Paris 2024 Olympics. The Wicklow woman had given birth to her third daughter less than six months before. Fionnuala is the first Irish woman to qualify for – wait for it – FIVE successive Olympic games. Her events have included the 3000m steeplechase, the 5000m and 10,000m.

4th December 1830

Countess Marguerite of Blessington returned to London and launched her literary salon. The Tipperary woman had lived in Europe with her husband but moved to London after his death. She supported herself and her partner, Count d'Orsay, by writing articles and fiction. She was renowned for her wit and intelligence, and her home was a gathering place for the London literati.

5th December 1995

Veronica Guerin was announced as a winner of the 1995 International Press Freedom Award. The Dublin journalist was fearless in her pursuit of the truth behind organised crime. She received multiple death threats but refused to be intimidated. In June 1996, she was shot and killed in her car while stopped at a traffic light. Her murder caused unprecedented national outrage.

6th December 1922

The Constitution of the Irish Free State, Bunreacht na hÉireann, gave the vote to all women over the age of twenty-one. The constitution promised universal citizenship 'without distinction of sex' – though this idealism would quickly be eroded by conservatism and Church-driven male domination. But from this day on, Irish women held the vote as equal citizens.

7th December 2022

Two Irish women triumphed in the European Prize
for Women Innovators. Dr Ciara Clancy developed
her Beats Medical app to help Parkinson's patients,
including a 'beat' to improve their walking. Engineer
Niamh Donnelly created specialised robots to clear
hospitals and nursing homes of bacteria and superbugs.
Irish women entrepreneurs have consistently excelled in
this competition, driving positive change in the world.

8th December 1922

Alice Stopford Green was announced as one of
Ireland's four new women senators. The Kells historian
had lived for a time in London, but the treatment by
Britain of its colonies had made her strongly anti-
Imperialist. She lent Roger Casement the money to
buy the rifles that were landed at Howth in 1914. And
after her return to Dublin, her home would become a
meeting point for leading nationalists.

9th December 1967

Sr Dr Maura Lynch arrived in Angola, fresh from her medical training. Born in Youghal, County Cork, she would go on to work all her life in Africa – in Angola, then Uganda. During her thirty years in Uganda, she set up an operating theatre and specialised in obstetrics. She was awarded a unique Certificate of Residency for Life from the Ugandan government. Her patients called her *Nakimuli* or 'Beautiful Flower'.

10th December 1977

Máiread Maguire and Betty Williams were awarded the Nobel Peace Prize. The two women set up the grassroots movement Peace People in Northern Ireland, bringing together Catholics and Protestants. They organised a series of rallies both north and south of the border, calling for an end to the bloodshed. They gained huge international support, touring the US and addressing the UN in New York.

11th December 2022

Raidió na Gaeltachta began its series on Irish-language poet Máire Bhuí Ní Laoghaire. Máire lived in Cork in the late 1700s and 1800s. Her best-known poem is '*Cath Chéim an Fhia*' ('The Battle of Keimaneigh'), about a skirmish between locals and the British Army. Máire was unable to read or write in Irish or English, and her poems were passed on in the oral tradition.

12th December 1990

Marital rape was finally recognised as a crime in Ireland. The women's movement had campaigned on it for years. The first case – two years later – collapsed within minutes. It would be twelve years before a man would be found guilty of raping his wife.

13th December 1767

The 18th-century singer Rachael Baptist was lauded for a series of concerts in Kilkenny. She made her debut public performance in Dublin in 1750 and spent the next twenty years singing in theatres and pleasure gardens across Ireland and England. Sometimes known as 'the Black Siren', she was the first Irish woman of colour to achieve international fame.

14th December 1982

For the first time ever, there was an Irish Minister of State for Women's Affairs. Dublin TD Nuala Fennell was a prominent activist who had helped set up Dublin's first women's shelter. In her time as minister, she pushed through legislation that included abolishing the status of illegitimacy – an important step in tackling social prejudice at the time.

15th December 2020

A portrait of Edna O'Brien was unveiled at the National Gallery of Ireland on her ninetieth birthday. The Clare writer had been courting controversy since her debut, *The Country Girls*, which came out in 1960. It was banned outright, as were six of her other novels. Her writing was long recognised for its portrayal of real women and unapologetic attitude to sex. She wrote nineteen novels over her sixty-year career and once said that 'writing is my breathing'.

16th December 2016

Annalise Murphy was named *Irish Times* Sportswoman of the Year. This came after the sailor's silver medal at the Rio Olympics – and European gold a few years earlier. Annalise found sailing a physically demanding and tactical sport, and the wild Irish waters were great practice. Since retiring from sailing, she has taken up competitive cycling. You can't keep a good woman down.

17th December 2018

Professor of Palaeontology Maria McNamara confirmed that pterosaurs had four kinds of feathers, a finding which pushed back the origin of feathers by 70 million years. Born in Tipperary, Maria studied in Ireland and the US before becoming a geologist at the Burren Geopark. Now based in UCC, her more recent studies have shown that pterosaurs could change the colour of their feathers using melanin pigments. *mind blown*

18th December 2020

Coco's Law was passed by both Houses of the Oireachtas. It outlawed the sharing of intimate images without consent. Jackie Fox had campaigned for the law since her daughter Coco took her own life after years of relentless bullying. Since her success with Coco's Law here, Jackie has taken her fight against cyber-bullying to the European parliament.

19th December 1973

The Supreme Court of Ireland struck down the ban on importing or selling contraceptives. The case was brought by 27-year-old mother of four Mary McGee, who had been told that another pregnancy would endanger her life. She ordered spermicidal jelly from the UK, but it was seized by Irish Customs. The Supreme Court ruled that married couples could make private decisions about contraception. It was a landmark judgment for Irish women's rights.

20th December 1972

The Irish government finally passed a law making sixteen the minimum age for marriage. Before that, there was no statutory minimum. Common law held the age for boys to be fourteen and for girls, just twelve.

21st December 1922

Aleen Cust was the first woman to be awarded a veterinary diploma in Ireland or Britain. She had qualified more than twenty-five years earlier but, as a woman, couldn't practise in her own right. She joined a practice and was even made Galway's Veterinary Inspector. The local press didn't take it well, proclaiming, 'We can understand women educating themselves to tend women – but horses! Heavens!' Heavens, indeed.

22nd **December** 1849

The story of Famine victim Bridget O'Donnel was published in *The Illustrated London News*. The accompanying drawing of Bridget and her two children became an iconic Famine image. The family were evicted from their Clare home, losing two children to starvation. Meanwhile, the corn they had grown was harvested and sold by their landlord. Bridget's story was not unusual in Ireland at the time, but it being published in a major British newspaper was unprecedented.

23rd **December** 1919

The Sex Disqualification (Removal) Act finally allowed women to practise law and veterinary surgery and join the higher civil service. Women in Ireland and Britain could also sit on juries and join professional bodies. It was a watered-down version of the Women's Emancipation Bill, which was much more radical.

24th December 1916

Winifred Carney was released from prison after being interned following the Rising. From County Down, Winifred had joined the Irish Citizen Army as a skilled markswoman. She was the only woman with the group that took over the GPO. Later, she was fiercely critical of partition and the growing conservatism of the Irish government. She refused to accept a pension for her role in 1916, relenting just weeks before her death.

25th December 2023

Cork Penny Dinners provided Christmas dinner to more than a thousand people. Caitríona Twomey has been the driving force behind the charity for more than fifteen years, serving food to those who can't afford it, seven days a week. Their motto is 'We never judge, we serve'. Penny Dinners dates back to the Quaker soup kitchens of the Famine. People would pay a penny for a dinner of two pints of soup and half a loaf of bread.

26th December 1950

Maeve Brennan's short story 'The Holy Terror' was published in *Harper's Bazaar*. Maeve grew up in Dublin but moved to the US with her family at seventeen. She wrote for *Harper's* under fellow Irish woman Carmel Snow and then moved to *The New Yorker*, with a regular column called 'The Long-Winded Lady'. Her editor said she 'had a tongue that could clip a hedge, and a longshoreman's mouth', but 'to be around her was to see style being reinvented'.

27th December 1904

The Abbey Theatre had its first ever opening night,

which featured the play *Spreading the News* by co-founder Lady Augusta Gregory. The Galwegian writer had long wanted an Irish national theatre that produced Irish plays. She was widowed at forty and only then began writing for theatre and retelling Irish legends. She was prolific, producing dozens of plays, and became a leading figure in the Irish Literary Revival.

28th December 1918

Constance Markievicz was the first woman elected to British parliament. She refused her seat, opting instead to become Ireland's first female cabinet minister (and only the second in the world). Not short of a few bob, Constance turned up to her first meeting of Daughters of Ireland in a ballgown and tiara. Amending her wardrobe accordingly, she served as second-in-command at St. Stephen's Green during the Rising. She famously said, 'There can be no free women in an enslaved nation.'

29th December 1921

The six elected women TDs stood up one by one to oppose the Treaty. They included Kathleen Clarke, Mary MacSwiney and Margaret Pearse. With strong undertones of misogyny, many of their male counterparts derided the women for having nothing but their family connections to recommend them. But these women were well-informed, strongly idealistic republicans, and many had long been active in the suffragist and nationalist causes.

30th December 1961

Phyllis Clinch was announced as UCD's first (and only) female professor of botany. The Dubliner specialised in viruses that decimate crops like potatoes, tomatoes and sugar beets. Her pioneering research helped avoid food shortages and won her the Boyle Medal. She was the first woman to receive the accolade – and the only one until Margaret Murnane, an unbelievable fifty years later.

31st December 1891

The S.S. *Nevada* arrived into New York from Cobh, County Cork. Its passengers included seventeen-year-old Annie Murphy and her little brothers, travelling to reunite with their parents. The following morning, Annie was the first person to pass through the new Ellis Island immigration station. Newly designed software that helps match refugees with their ideal resettlement location is called 'Annie' in her honour.

About the Author

Kunak McGann is the author of *A Hundred Words for Grand*, *Red Rover, Red Rover!* and, with Sarah Cassidy, *Ah … That's Gas!*, *The A to Z of an Irish Christmas*, *The A to Z of Being Irish* and *Irish Mammy in Your Pocket*. She works in publishing and lives in Kildare with her husband, two lively sons and one chilled-out dog.

Also by Kunak McGann

A Hundred Words for Grand: The Little Book of Irish Chat

How to win friends and influence people, Irish style! A collection words and phrases to showcase the famed Irish gift of the gab, from fond greetings and terms of endearment to slaps on the back and typically understated compliments.

Red Rover, Red Rover! Games from an Irish Childhood (That You Can Teach Your Kids)

With easy instructions, handy tips and 'risk ratings', this book will whisk you back to those carefree days of childhood and, if your creaky old bones are up to it, inspire you to get out with the kids and revel in those games all over again.

By Kunak McGann
& Sarah Cassidy

Find out more at obrien.ie

Enjoying life with

Hundreds of books
for all occasions

From beautiful gifts to books you won't
want to be parted from! Great writing,
beautiful illustration and leading design.
Discover books for readers of all ages.

Follow us for all the latest news and
information, or go to our website
to explore our full range of titles.

 TheOBrienPress   TheOBrienPress

 OBrienPress   TheOBrienPress

Visit, explore, buy
obrien.ie